THE CHALLENGES TO DEMOCRACY

THE *Challenges* TO DEMOCRACY

CONSENSUS AND EXTREMISM IN AMERICAN POLITICS

by Murray Clark Havens

UNIVERSITY OF TEXAS PRESS AUSTIN

Printed by the University of Texas Printing Division, Austin
Bound by Universal Bookbindery, Inc., San Antonio

TO AGNES

INTRODUCTION

This volume is intended for semipopular consumption. This is said, not by way of apology, but as a means of indicating partially its purpose and its method and its scope. I hope that my work will gain approval among my fellow scholars and that they will find it compatible with their own standards of scholarship. However, I did not undertake this study with the thought of my fellow political scientists as its primary audience. Instead, I planned it to serve a broader group of interested and literate readers who wish to learn about the phenomena described here, not as professional analysts but as concerned citizens. The health of the political system, after all, is of importance not merely to professional politicians, political scientists, and historians. It is vital to all the people, and those people, in turn, determine in large part just how healthy our society will be. My intention is to enable each of them to make his contribution to this end with greater awareness of the importance of certain aspects of the American political system and greater understanding of the nature of some challenges to the stability of that system.

It is with these considerations in mind that I have tried to avoid the technical vocabulary of modern political science and to employ language with which the educated layman is already familiar. Where a technical term must be employed because there is no adequate substitute, I have attempted to explain its meaning clearly in nontechnical terms. This is not to suggest that the book's target is the proverbial "man in the street." But college students, bright high school seniors, and similarly educated and informed readers off the campus, it is hoped, will find the language readable and the concepts intelligible.

This book was begun in the immediate aftermath of the assassination of President John F. Kennedy. That tragic event raised for the author, as for many other observers, serious questions as to the permanance of some of the patterns we had associated with American government. Most of us had thought of the United States as a society possessed of unusual unity and political stability, as well as liberty and material prosperity for most of its members. As a nation we had prided ourselves on our orderliness and our respect for the rule of law. We had been both amused and annoyed at countries where governmental instability through revolution, mob violence, military coup d'etat, and political assassination had been endemic, and we had referred a little contemptuously to their apparent inability to adopt more orderly techniques for achieving political goals. After November 22, 1963, it became necessary to re-examine this assessment. Kennedy was the fourth American President in less than a century to be murdered while in office. Were these tragedies symptomatic of something fundamental in American society? (During that century, and for a long time before, not a single British monarch or prime minister had been similarly killed.) Was our relatively tranquil recent history the product as much of fortuitous circumstances as of basic elements in our society? Was our history really that tranquil? Were past internal conflicts not merely isolated historical incidents but part of a repetitive pattern through which our national unity might be in continuing jeopardy? Were current conflicts involving race relations, civil liberties, and the so-called radical right part of such a pattern, or were they isolated phenomena peculiar to our own time? In either case, how serious was the threat posed by these developments? All of these questions seemed to demand answers before we could be sure of dealing effectively with the problem of political stability in our country.

The particular focus of this inquiry is the nature of American political unity and the challenges to that unity. Attention is given first to the theoretical concept of political obligation and consensus. When the general conditions under which national cohesion is feasible are understood it is possible to consider the particular factors which have produced such unity in the United States. What are the elements which have brought us together in the past? Which of these are still relevant? How effective are these cohesive forces in the situation in which we find ourselves today? When these questions have been answered we can move on to analysis of the individuals and groups falling outside the pattern of American consensus at various times during our history. There have been many of these, and each of them constituted the political extremism of a particular time. Some of them were politically insignificant and posed no serious threat to our governmental institutions and processes, although they were no doubt annoying enough to other people at the time. On the other hand, some were real and obvious dangers which were surmounted only with great difficulty. Only by the narrowest of margins, for example, did we survive as a nation the ordeal of the Civil War. Some of the challenges to the American consensus were based on considerations of a sort which most of us would now regard as possessing a high measure of ethical validity, although we may still criticize the means which were employed to advance those causes. (The abolitionist movement would, for many of us, fall into this category.) Other movements strike the average American of the 1960's as defenses of absurd positions from the beginning. Whatever its character, each of these had to be dealt with in one way or another. Had any one of these challenges been successful, the pattern of American development would have been greatly different. Some of them, if successful, would have modified the very elements which to many of us make America worthwhile.

The most important aspect of this study is an examination of the contemporary political scene in the United States. The term "political extremism" has been employed with regard to several movements during recent years. Some of these do constitute at least potential threats to the consensus which has been the basis of our national unity. Some openly deny that their members are obligated in any degree to support a government which is guilty of serious violations of what they regard as the most important of moral principles. Citizens ought not to be loyal, the leaders of these groups argue, to a society which is itself disloyal to standards which they believe to be good, right, and just.

It is with these challenges to American democracy—both theoretical and real, both past and current—that this book deals. It is as well to indicate here that I believe that our democracy has considerable potential for survival. Perhaps I believe it even more strongly after writing this book. Nor do I hold that belief only on the basis of faith in the merits of democracy, although that faith is present. The course of American history suggests that the national commitment to democracy is relatively deep and quite real. The commitment to American nationalism is even deeper. Given favorable circumstances, including an awareness of the dangers represented by political extremism, those commitments should prevail against any foreseeable internal threats. The purpose of this book is to aid in producing those circumstances.

ACKNOWLEDGMENTS

I am indebted to a sizable army of fellow scholars who, through their writing, their teaching, or their conversation, have enriched my understanding of the nature of American democracy and the foundations of national unity in the United States. A book such as this is obviously dependent on the technical contributions of many other men, for no one analyst can possibly explore at first hand all of the ramifications of a field as broad as this aspect of politics. I have tried to give to those writers proper credit through appropriate entries in the Bibliography, but many have no doubt been neglected, including some, I am sure, whose influence, though significant, was not consciously recognized as such even at the time.

I am also indebted to the Anti-Defamation League of B'nai B'rith and to the Hogg Foundation for Mental Health for grants which enabled me to undertake the development of this book. Oscar Cohen and Theodore Freedman deserve special thanks for their generous assistance. Neither the Hogg Foundation nor the Anti-Defamation League has attempted to influence my conclusions, which are exclusively my own responsibility.

Many colleagues at the University of Texas assisted in this venture through discussion of these topics and through some strenuous arguments about them. Their critical views were of great importance in the development of my own ideas. Three fellow members of the Department of Government—William S. Livingston, Wallace Mendelson, and Emmette S. Redford—read extensive sections of the manuscript. Their comments and suggestions were especially appreciated, including those which the author declined to use—depriving himself, in the process, of his only opportunity to evade responsibility for the book's defects.

CONTENTS

THE CHALLENGES TO DEMOCRACY

1. The Nature of Political Obligation

*P*olitical obligation is a subject that has fascinated political theorists and philosophers since men first began to think about politics in a systematic way. What are the relations between a man and his country or society? What duties, if any, does he owe to his country? What is the ethical justification for the obligations which he owes to his country and to his fellow citizens? What obligations, if any, do they owe to him? What are the factors which actually hold a society together? Under what circumstances do these elements fail to do so? Are there ever circumstances under which an individual or a group of individuals is justified in acting politically in a way contrary to their normal obligations? If so, what are those circumstances? These are some of the fundamental questions with which political philosophy and political science have to deal. They are extraordinarily difficult questions to answer. To some of them no completely satisfactory answers have been found. To others a variety of answers is available, some of which contradict others. All of this is very annoying; yet these questions are so crucial that we can not avoid them. Those who refuse to deal directly with them nevertheless answer them by implication, but since they do not really understand either the answers or their consequences, they are often quite unhappy about those consequences at a later time.

The aim of this book is to enable its readers to understand what is involved in these questions of political obligation. No absolute answers will be provided, because such answers must always, in the last analysis, be personal, but the consequences of some of the possible answers will be explored, as will some of the elements that help to hold American society together and some of the factors which threaten its basic unity. Those who recognize these principles, even though they disagree with each other (and with this author) on many other things, have learned how to draw the line between those matters on which controversy and conflict are permissible and even desirable and those on which such conflict jeopardizes the survival of the nation and its political system.

Theories of Political Obligation

Some theories of political obligation are clearly theological in origin. The will of God is their basic ethical support. In some of these theories, such as those supporting the divine right of kings, God imposes on man obligations toward his country and its sovereign, but these are not dependent on any benefits he may derive from his fellow citizens or the monarch. There is obligation, all right, but it is strictly a one-way relationship. No matter how desperate his situation, the subject must obey his sovereign and never rebel, and he must do this simply because God has so commanded. On the other hand, there have been theories of obligation, also oriented toward religion, which were less one-sided. The subject was still obligated to obey his sovereign, but the sovereign had duties too, and, as both he and his subjects were under God, the obligation was equally binding on both sides. This approach was typical of medieval political thinkers. It raised an obvious question, however. What happened if the monarch ignored his responsibilities? Was he still entitled to the obedience of his subjects? Some authorities thought that he was and that his malfeasance by no means excused disloyalty among others. His punishment would be up to God. Others taught that the claim of the king upon the loyalty of his subjects was dependent upon his own conduct toward them. If the ruler governed badly and without reference to the needs and well-being of those under his rule, they might properly refuse to obey him. Under extreme circumstances, according to a few writers, a tyrant might even be murdered, in order to restore just government.

Closely related to the proposition that the individual was obligated to obey his king was the argument that he was obligated to obey the law. Of course, if the law simply reflected the king's will, the two cases were identical. But law was seldom thought to be this simple. In many countries the ruler was considered to be the discoverer or proclaimer of the law but not really its maker. The true origin of the law was variously held to be either God or nature or the traditions of a particular people. Man-made law, whether made by the king himself or by some legislative body, was primarily for the purpose of implementing the "natural law" and was valid only so long as it did not conflict with "natural law," whatever its origin. The individual was obligated to obey those laws which were valid by this standard, but he was free, indeed he was morally required, to disobey others. The problem, of course, was in trying to determine the content of natural law—a task that has produced conflict among able thinkers for many centuries. It is usually by reference to this sort of "higher law" that critics of particular laws justify disobeying them. It is the statute itself which is evil, they argue, not its violation.

Beginning with the seventeenth century, a new approach to the problem of political obligation began to attract a great deal of attention. The old natural-law arguments could sometimes be detected in it, but its emphasis was not on God but on man. This approach, of which the most prominent spokesmen were Thomas Hobbes, John Locke, and Jean Jacques Rousseau, made use of the device of "the social contract." Although very great differences existed among these three political philosophers (and some less well-known thinkers who used the same device), all three stressed that political obligation is necessary because without it life for all men becomes much more difficult and less pleasant—perhaps even impossible. It was the alternative consequences for men which made political obligation a necessity.

For Hobbes the practical consequences of this approach were very similar to those resulting from divine-right theory. In the absence of strong government, civilized society—perhaps even life itself—is out of the question. Therefore such government is necessary, no matter how brutal or tyrannical it may become in the hands of a particular ruler, for it is still better than the anarchy that prevails without it. The subject is obligated to obey the ruler; the ruler has no obligation except to rule forcefully and effectively. Rebellion, therefore, cannot be justified. This is not a pleasant philosophy, which is one reason why it never became popular. Yet this is not at all times a pleasant world, and those who are forced actually to regard the alternative of civil strife and a complete collapse of governmental and social institutions may well discover a great deal of merit in Hobbes' forceful logic.

In a situation which is not quite so desperate, John Locke is perhaps more appealing, for his contract between the ruler and the ruled involved duties on both sides. True, a legitimate ruler ought to be obeyed, and those who refused to obey him might properly be punished. But he was obligated to rule not only forcefully but also justly, and against an unjust ruler or tyrant, who was actually the breaker of the social contract, there was a right of revolution. Locke was actually writing in order to justify such a revolution—that which exiled James II in 1688. (Locke was not the only great political philosopher who began as a political propagandist.) Naturally enough, when Americans a century later were seeking to justify a revolution of their own, it was Locke whose arguments they employed. They were not promoting anarchy and certainly were not denying the existence of duties toward one's country and one's government. They simply argued that in the particular circumstances of unjust British rule, under which they were denied rights they regarded as fundamental, it was proper to rebel, not to promote anarchy but to establish a new government which would better deserve their loyalty.

The doctrine of political obligation found in Rousseau is much more complex than the theories of Hobbes and of Locke. Rousseau's philosophy in general is very difficult to understand, and it can be interpreted in many different ways. It can be construed as supporting democracy. It can also be viewed as the foundation of modern totalitarianism. The former view is of significance here. Rousseau's direct impact on the United States was very limited, but the notion that it is possible to relate the concept of political obligation to a role for the public in determining the nature of that obligation was to be very important for this country, and Rousseau was at least partly responsible for the development of that idea. The other theorists mentioned here assumed the existence of a monarchy in constructing their theories, although it is true that some of their ideas, especially those of Locke and Hobbes, could be readily adapted to other circumstances. Rousseau found this assumption unnecessary, and his doctrine stands without reference to a monarch. The public could, he insisted, create its own obligation.

All the theories of political obligation that have been discussed so far are ethical or "normative" theories—that is, they are statements of how men *ought* to act in relation to their ruler or their country, either because God, nature, or tradition so demanded, or because life for all members of the society would become more difficult or even intolerable otherwise. It is also possible to examine this problem from another standpoint, which is more or less removed from the question of ethics. Employing this approach, one ignores the question of what obligations men ought to have and looks instead for the obligations which men behave as if they had. What loyalties do men actually possess? How do those loyalties develop? What happens when an individual holds two loyalties which come into conflict? What happens when large groups of individuals find themselves in this position? It is impossible really to understand the political character of any country unless one has inquired into some of these questions as they apply to that country. Much of the analysis in this study consists of efforts to deal with these questions in the context of the United States, both today and at crucial points in our earlier history.

The argument of this book does not depend on acceptance of any particular one of these theories. For that matter, the author himself does not find any of them completely satisfactory. But the analysis will not be meaningful to anyone who rejects entirely *all* notions of political obligation. The extreme individualist—the man who denies that he has any obligations except to himself and to his family—is likely to find this book absurd, for such a man is an anarchist, and this is a book about government. Furthermore, much of the book is about democratic government, and even though many of its comments will be valid for other systems as well, anyone who completely rejects the democratic insistence on ultimate governmental responsibility to the public is bound to find much of the book unsatisfactory.

Political Obligation and Democracy

Democracy is a rather tricky word. Clarification of just what it means, as well as of some of the things which it does not mean, at least for the purposes of this book, is essential to intelligent use of it in this analysis. The word *democracy* as used here does not mean direct government by the entire public. The town meeting is a noble institution, but even at the local level government by the people is not as simple as many romanticized impressions would have us believe. For an entire nation, particularly one as large as the United States, any attempt by the public as a whole to determine policies directly and then to carry them out without the use of specialized governmental institutions is clearly absurd. Policy making requires time which most members of the public do not have. It requires expert knowledge which they have had little opportunity to obtain. It requires the balancing of many complex considerations. And even when a policy decision has been reached, administering it may prove to be an even more difficult task.

These two jobs are assigned in a democracy to two much criti-cized but absolutely essential professions—the politicians and the bureaucrats. Our political system could not conceivably work in the absence of either of them. It is the politicians who provide leadership for the system. It is they, guided in substantial part by the expertise of the professional civil servants, who make the important policy decisions for the country. It is they who supervise the administration of those policies, although that administration is handled in detail by those same civil servants. And it is the politicians again who provide the major line of communication between the public and the government.

If the people do not govern, what is their role in a democracy? What is the difference between democracy and its alternatives? One answer, of course, is that in a democracy the people select their own political leaders. This would be correct, as far as it goes, for one of the criteria of democracy is certainly the existence of free elections, but this is still a little too simple. For one thing, the voters usually have only the limited alternatives made available to them by the political parties. Furthermore, this leaves it unclear what influence the electoral process may have on the making and administration of policies. If changes in personnel produce no other results, it is doubtful that the process is worthwhile, except to the winning candidates.

The true significance of elections is that they are the most important device, though by no means the only one, through which the public may indicate to the government its basic needs and demands. We must beware of the assumption that an election result indicates a national commitment to a particular policy line. Few voters cast their ballots on the basis of any one specific issue, and many of them do so without regard for any issues at all. But the public does indicate through election results whether or not it is generally satisfied with the direction in which the government is moving and the effectiveness with which it is going there. The re-election of a President and most of his political supporters, for example, is an indication that most of the American people are fairly well satisfied with the performance of their government, especially if that re-election is by a substantial margin. A less emphatic victory suggests that at least a large minority is unhappy with significant elements of the situation, and actual defeat obviously means that a majority wants changes.

What will actually happen on the basis of these results is, of course, up to the political leaders, whether new or re-elected. It may well be that programs about which the public is unhappy simply cannot be modified. In some fields, particularly those of foreign policy and national defense, the limits of practical policy are often quite narrow, and the alternatives may be so limited that a change in national leadership produces surprisingly few new policies in these areas. If this is the case, the task of political leadership may be the education of the public to the value of the old policies. On the other hand, there are times when new programs really can be implemented, and under those circumstances public dissatisfaction with old arrangements ought to be the signal for some new departures.

The heart of democracy is the proposition that people, in the last analysis, are the best judges of their own interests. They may not know, in terms of specific policies, how to advance those interests, but they can be depended on to indicate whether the situation in general is one which they find tolerable. It is for this reason that arguments for restricting the suffrage to a limited part of the population are defective. If voting were really the process of determining public policy, such restriction might be necessary. Indeed, the number of people really qualified to make policies for a govern-

10

ment as complex as ours is so small that democracy would be altogether impossible under such circumstances. But since the real function of elections is simply to indicate whether or not past policies are acceptable for the present, the only qualification necessary is the ability to tell when one is being hurt and then to squawk loudly—by voting for candidates of the party which has been out of office.

Democracy alters the basis of political obligation. The superficial argument that one is bound to obey those laws which one has helped to make need not concern us here. The fact remains that within the democratic framework, through the established political system, an opportunity to do something about the current situation is available for those who are unhappy about existing political arrangements. It is much harder to justify rebellion and disobedience when this is the case. If the individual was eligible to vote but failed to do so, he can hardly blame the rest of the society for his lost chance. If he voted but found himself in a minority, he can scarcely demand that a larger part of the population give up the protection of their interests in order to defend his; nor can he claim that he owes them no loyalty if they do not make such a sacrifice. (If he does claim that, he is back with our friends the anarchists again.) If he voted with the majority but finds that his interests are still suffering, it may have been because the complaints and demands of the rest of that majority were not the same as his. If they did share his views, the men whom they placed in office may have found that the programs in question could not be modified without producing an even less acceptable situation. (The charge that the leaders of *both* parties ignore the needs of the public is nonsense; no politician enjoys losing an election.)

The above analysis presumes, of course, that a genuine democratic regime is operating and that the opportunity to influence it in the manner indicated here is available to all of the significant elements within the society. If political obligation is reinforced by democracy, it is reinforced only for those who can participate in

11

the democracy. Any individual or group which is denied the opportunity to vote, or whose votes are not counted, or which is prevented in any other way from exercising the same political influence as that possessed by the remainder of the society can scarcely be expected to give to that society the sort of loyalty that it can expect from others. If there is any political obedience due from such a group, we must go back to thinkers like Hobbes and the divine-right theorists to give it intellectual support, for it obtains none from democratic theory.

There is also a situation in which someone who does participate fully in a democratic society and who believes in democracy and who admits that he is in general obligated toward that society may nevertheless decide that he cannot obey one or more important decisions made in that society. The duty of civil disobedience (which may also be invoked by those who are denied political rights) is usually affirmed when a subject of extreme moral significance enters the political arena. Anyone who believes that there are some absolute ethical principles on which no compromise ought to be permitted is committed in theory to civil disobedience, although he may never be put to the test unless his principles become political issues. Even then he has no problem unless he winds up on the losing side of one of these political struggles.

The duty to disobey has been urged on occasion by men of great courage and high moral purpose, such as Thoreau, Gandhi, and Socrates. Nevertheless, it is a profoundly disrupting force, and we must recognize that any society in which it is used on frequent occasions by many different elements is unlikely to retain stability or even a minimum of unity. Anyone whose religious or ethical beliefs suggest to him the need to refuse to go along with a particular political decision ought to consider carefully whether the issue in question is important enough to warrant jeopardizing the capacity of the society to deal successfully with a large number of future problems. Only if the issue at hand outweighs in importance all of the other political problems of which one can conceive is one seemingly justified in contesting a decision which has been made in final form by the legitimate processes of a democratic society. He must, in other words, be fighting for something which is so important to him that it is worth the risk of disunity and even anarchy.

The principle of political obligation does not limit the free exchange of political ideas, which is vital to democracy. Criticism remains perfectly possible. The obligation to obey laws and to help to carry out policies of which one disapproves does not preclude efforts to change them. A democratic country in which there is no dissent and no disagreement is a country which is not doing anything important. But it is possible for loyal men to dissent and for good citizens to disagree, both before the establishment of a given policy and after it has been placed in operation. The proper line to be drawn is that between criticism and sabotage. Attempts to use the democratic process to secure changes in public policy must be tolerated and protected. Attempts to prevent the carrying out of those policies while they are in effect cannot be permitted. A democratic nation is not required to secure unanimous consent before it acts. If necessary, it can act over the vigorous and even violent objections of a sizable minority, so long as that minority is accorded the right to participate and legitimately to protest against the action to which it is opposed.

Political Obligation in the American Setting

Democracy adds to the force of political obligation in this country, but it is certainly not the only factor which impels Americans to behave as if they were Americans. In this country, as in many others, an important motivation is to be found in nationalism. A common conviction that we are Americans and that this common identification with our country is something extremely important characterizes most inhabitants of the United States. In some ways, this is one of the most amazing things about this country. Our unity persists despite the fact that we are one of the largest countries in the world, both in land area and in popula-

13

tion. Both our population and our economic activities are of highly diversified character. The variety of racial, ethnic, and religious groupings represented in our population can be matched scarcely anywhere else in the world. Developing and maintaining unity among them has not been easy, but it has been done. The many pressures tending to tear our society apart have been contained—though never eliminated completely—and the forces promoting unity have remained dominant. But what are those forces?

One is democracy itself. A common commitment to the democratic pattern has been shared by most of the American people for the better part of two centuries. Dissenters from this view have always been among us, and at the beginning of our history they were quite numerous, but our basic determination to maintain governmental responsibility to the public has always been clear. In addition, the size of that public has steadily increased, and each step adding another element to the ranks of those exercising political influence has met with the approval of a majority of those who already possessed such influences. We have believed that every group could be made responsible citizens of our country, and we have accomplished a great deal on the basis of that belief.

A second unifying force, by no means peculiar to the United States, has been nationalism. Unlike most European countries, America did not develop its national identity out of an effort to overthrow or limit a monarch (for, despite its propaganda, our revolution was against Great Britain, not George III). Nor were we constantly forced to reassert our independence against a host of adjacent threatening states. On the contrary, it never occurred to most Americans from the end of the American Revolution until well into the twentieth century that events anywhere else in the world could have an effect on this country, much less influence its capacity to survive. The United States had a history much more like that of some of the present newly independent nations of Asia and Africa. Gaining independence by throwing off colonial rule,

14

we found that the chief opposition to nationalism was not an external power but internal disunity and its spokesmen. The threat of that disunity we have had to counter time and time again, once through an extraordinarily bloody civil war and many times through bitter political fights, and we are still called on to counter it today.

Part of the strength of American nationalism came from the intense conviction of many Americans during the nineteenth century that our future was bound to be a glorious one. It was our "manifest destiny" to rule a continent, and we came close to doing so. With abundant empty spaces into which to expand, with the resources to support a population many times greater than we had, with millions of potential immigrants anxious to help us to fill those spaces and exploit those resources, and with no strong neighbors anxious to contest our right to do so, few apparent limitations restricted the future of America. Loyalty to a society which was so obviously on the way up was not difficult to promote. In the middle of the twentieth century this invincible self-confidence was to lead us into difficulties, for we were to discover that, great as our power might be, some things we still could not accomplish. But in an earlier time, having the courage of our convictions paid off.

The relatively high standard of living of the American people also contributed to national unity and political stability. Our economic well-being was dependent in part on the extremely rapid expansion of an economy which could not continue to expand at the same rate forever and in part on the exploitation of natural resources which would be difficult or impossible for later generations to replace, but, for well over a century, these problems did not concern us very much. True, certain elements in our population seldom shared in this prosperity, and at times most of our population had economic troubles, but for the politically influential parts of the American citizenry those times were spaced at relatively wide intervals and were usually rather brief. As a result, the desperate economic circumstances that might have made most Americans seek relief in almost any political direction, including disunity, seldom existed.

Another aspect of the American political scene was the tendency of many Americans to avoid politics altogether, if possible. This was in part a product of our happy economic situation. Politics and economics did not remain separate, and most of our political controversies have actually been rooted in economic matters, but those controversies were usually not of life-and-death importance to those involved in them. On the whole we found it possible to reach pragmatic and nondoctrinaire solutions to those problems—solutions which usually proved fully satisfactory to very few but relatively tolerable to almost all. Conflict along economic lines which would more profoundly disturb the political equilibrium did not develop until the twentieth century, with its more serious economic problems, the increase in political influence for those who had always been at the bottom of the economic ladder, and the more readily awakened consciences of those in more fortunate circumstances.

Our success in maintaining a relatively high degree of national unity over almost two centuries is no proof that such unity will always and inevitably be present. There are, after all, many, many things on which Americans disagree, and some of those disagreements have political significance. The vast majority of them, of course, represent no denial of political obligation and pose no threat to the basic consensus within our society. Once during our history that consensus failed completely for a time. On other occasions it has been jeopardized, and a number of potential threats to it can be found today. The purpose of this book is to analyze the more serious of these failures and potential failures, past and present, and to describe their consequences in terms of the survival of this country and of the kind of American society in which most of us want to live.

2. The Healthy Political System

What is a healthy political system? For what symptoms does the political pathologist look when he suspects that a society is unhealthy? What are the causes of the ailments to which the body politic may be prone? What do we mean when we say that a society is sound or unsound? These are questions which must be answered before we can attempt to decide what, if anything, is wrong with the American political system and what, if anything, ought to be done about it. It is possible, of course, to answer all of these questions strictly in terms of the personal preferences of the individual observer, who may say that a healthy or sound political system is one which accomplishes the purposes of which he approves, especially if the system seems likely to continue to accomplish his goals. This is the sort of answer which the social scientist calls "value-oriented," meaning that the answer will make sense only to other people who share some of the basic attitudes. Almost everyone does most of his thinking about politics in these value-oriented terms. There is nothing "wrong" (in the sense of "immoral") with this approach, but for our purposes it is necessary to go a little further and to develop answers which will be meaningful even for opposing groups of people who disagree about some of the particular goals which they would like the political system to accomplish.

The ultimate symptom of political disease is revolution, which is an indication that at least a significant element of the population is so dissatisfied with the performance of the existing governmental system that its elimination seems preferable to its continuation. But the political pathologist examining a successful revolution is really conducting a post-mortem examination of a pattern of government. Regretfully, this is sometimes necessary, both in political science and in medicine. Some historians incline to the view that neither societies nor men are immortal and that sooner or later each disappears from the scene. Even if this be the case, many of us would like to postpone the inevitable for our own society, and this makes it necessary for us to learn to recognize less drastic indications that something is wrong with the political process and to diagnose the particular difficulty that may be present. Unfortunately, this is not a simple task, for the most dangerous political ailments are often the most difficult to diagnose, while the most alarming symptoms are sometimes related to essentially non-malignant conditions. Despite these problems, political scientists have progressed a long way toward agreement as to some of the circumstances in which an optimistic prognosis can be delivered. They also know some of the conditions in which the survival of a particular set of political institutions becomes doubtful.

Agreement on the Fundamental Character of the System

One necessity in a viable system of government is general agreement regarding the fundamental character of that system itself. This agreement need not be universal, but it must include all the elements which are seriously capable of disrupting the system. If there are significant groups, measured either by their numbers or by their key positions within the society, which refuse to accept as legitimate the constitutional arrangements of

18

that society, those arrangements will always be in jeopardy. With one exception, we have had no serious struggles over the constitutional structure of the United States. That exception was the Civil War, in which one of the two major issues was the relationship between the national government and the states. The implications of that conflict will be examined in greater detail later, but it was obviously the most serious crisis that this country has yet survived. Perhaps good fortune accounts in part for the failure of similar constitutional crises to develop at other points in American history. There have been, after all, other fundamental questions on which Americans have disagreed.

The American Revolution could itself have become the occasion of further dissension after the end of the fighting. American opinion was by no means unanimous on the subject of separation from the British Empire. Rough estimates suggest that as many as one-third of the inhabitants of the thirteen colonies were opposed to independence, with another group of about equal size indifferent. Some of the bloodiest fighting of the war involved Americans on both sides. Nevertheless, this conflict ceased with the end of British participation in the war. No simple explanation of the development of American nationalism between 1763 and 1789 is possible, but a partial answer is to be found in the large-scale emigration of the American Tories (and particularly their leaders) to Canada and other parts of the British Empire. The group which would have been most inclined to reject the new regime was no longer in the country. Furthermore, British acceptance of the fact of independence in 1783 left American supporters of the crown in the position of wanting a monarch who no longer wanted them. In addition, although the American Revolution did have more in the way of social and economic consequences than some historians have been willing to recognize, it certainly did not produce the sort of social upheaval which developed in France after 1789. Even those opposed to independence found that most of the social institutions to which they were accustomed were, at least in the

19

short run, relatively unchanged. (Over the next century and three-quarters extremely important changes did take place, albeit gradually.) Whatever the causes, there was never a serious attempt to undo the work of 1776. Like the Glorious Revolution a century earlier in Britain, the American Revolution was largely immune from subsequent challenge as the source of legitimacy of the regime.

The benefits we have gained from this acceptance of the American Revolution are clearest if we compare our situation with that of France. The French Revolution took place at about the same time as ours. Its ideology was in part copied from ours. Yet the French Revolution was never accepted as final, whereas the American Revolution had acquired that status within a few years of its conclusion. France has always had significant groups dedicated to the proposition that the events of 1789 were evil and that the political and social consequences of the French Revolution ought, if possible, to be reversed. The republican form of government has by no means gained the approval of the entire French population. As late as 1875 a majority of that population probably supported monarchy, and even today overt opposition to the republican regime characterizes a significant minority (even if the Communists be listed among the dedicated supporters of republican government, a proposition which is open not only to doubt but to ridicule). With support from a fair number of Frenchmen, the authoritarian Pétain government during World War II dropped the republican "Liberty, Equality, Fraternity" from official usage and replaced it with "Work, Family, Fatherland." Americans quarrel enough about the precise meaning of our eighteenth-century revolutionary language, but we have seldom had to battle those who would alter the wording itself, or the basic character of the regime which it was employed to support.

The writing and adoption of the Constitution might have provided another occasion for fundamental American disunity. During the last decade of the eighteenth century a significant part of the American population, after narrowly failing in its efforts to prevent ratification of the new document in such key states as Virginia and New York, continued to question its acceptability. Two serious complaints were made by these critics, led by such noted figures as Patrick Henry, George Clinton, and Richard Henry Lee. The first concerned the division of powers between state and national governments. The second involved their demand for democracy.

Devoted to the principle of state sovereignty and relatively well satisfied with the arrangements under the Articles of Confederation, which reflected that principle, Henry and his colleagues saw no need to modify those arrangements so as to reduce the powers of the states. On the contrary, they felt that any defects which might have developed during the period the Articles had been in effect could be corrected by the individual states or by voluntary co-operation among groups of states, without the necessity of transferring fundamental authority to the national level.

Although the supporters of the Constitution did manage to achieve its ratification, the Anti-Federalists resolved to continue the struggle, and their protests against the new constitutional arrangements were quite vociferous through the 1790's, reaching their high point in the Virginia and Kentucky Resolutions of 1798, proclaiming that the Constitution was only a compact among still sovereign states. This particular aspect of the controversy died down with the election of Jefferson as President in 1800. He had been the most important leader of the Anti-Federalists and had indeed been the author of the Kentucky Resolutions. To the great disappointment of those of his followers who had assumed that his election heralded the end of the doctrine of national supremacy, Jefferson as President did not undertake to reduce the role of the national government to the limited functions spelled out literally in the Constitution. His inaugural address, with the words, "We are all republicans—we are all federalists," served notice that Jefferson considered the Constitution the settled basis for American

21

government and the union a permanent one. Despite his continuing verbal commitment to the strict construction of the powers delegated to the national government, Jefferson acted on a number of matters—notably foreign policy and the acquisition of Louisiana—in a fashion scarcely to be supported by a narrow interpretation of national powers. Having no political alternative to supporting their erstwhile hero, of whose actual policies most of them still approved, the former spokesmen for state sovereignty were for the most part silent. For many of them, and probably for Jefferson himself, despite some of his earlier statements which seem to imply the contrary, the powers of the states were of significance only in an instrumental sense. As long as a defense of those powers seemed to Jefferson to be the most likely device for achieving the humanitarian and libertarian goals he valued most highly, he was as zealous as any man in defending the states from national encroachment. Once it became clear to him, especially after his own election to the Presidency, that the national government could also be employed to accomplish those ends, Jefferson began to place much less emphasis on state powers.

The decline in the controversy over the place of the states in the American political system during the first quarter of the nineteenth century was only temporary, of course. Its return after 1830 was far more serious and was ultimately to be settled by violence. The relationship of the Civil War to the nature of American government was quite complex and will be discussed in some detail later in this study. For the moment, it is enough to note that the war was only in part a war about states' rights. There certainly were some people in Southern states to whom the abstraction of the powers of their state was important enough to command their loyalties even to the point of war, just as there were those in the North (and quite a few in the South as well) to whom the similar abstraction of national sovereignty was equally important. But these abstractions cannot be considered by themselves, for there were many other people to whom the abstractions were less important than the goals to be accomplished through them. Reversing the way in which Jefferson had tended to forget his earlier dedication to state sovereignty when he became President, the foremost spokesman for state sovereignty during the quarter century after Jefferson's death—John C. Calhoun—was a convert from ardent nationalism. This change was not perhaps unrelated to Calhoun's growing realization that ends vital to himself and to his constituents, including free trade, Southern economic expansion, and the defense of slavery, might not indefinitely be protected by a national government which would not always be dominated by the relatively sparsely populated South. Hidden behind the controversies over states' rights and national powers are two questions which are always important but which are too seldom explicitly answered: States' rights to do *what*? National powers to do *what*?

The Civil War did provide what has been, through the present time, the definitive answer to the problem of the locus of sovereignty in this country. It resides in the nation, not the separate states. A decision which could not be made through ordinary legal processes could be obtained through that "extension of politics by other means" which we call war and could then be recognized as binding by a Supreme Court which was to refer in an important decision shortly after Appomattox to "the late wicked rebellion." The wording of Article VI of the Constitution, clear enough to some of its readers from the beginning, had been made politically effective:

This Constitution, and the Laws of the United States which shall be made in Pursuance thereof; and all Treaties made, or which shall be made, under the Authority of the United States, shall be the supreme Law of the Land; and the Judges in every State shall be bound thereby, any Thing in the Constitution or Laws of any State to the Contrary notwithstanding.

The struggle over the place of the states was not the only one to plague the new society. For quite some time after the adoption of the Constitution the basic nature of our government was un-decided in still another respect. This had been the second major objection of the critics of the Constitution. To those who believed strongly in democracy, the Constitution was a disappointment. Some of the opposition to its ratification stemmed from precisely this, although the issues of state authority and of democracy tended to become confused in the minds of some spokesmen for both—a problem which has not altogether disappeared 175 years later. The writers of the Constitution were not convinced of the merits of popular government. The trend toward more broadly based control of state governments was one of their more impor-tant reasons for desiring a stronger national government. They therefore wrote into the Constitution a number of provisions seem-ingly contrary to democratic principles. The indirect selection of the President and the Senate (the former by an electoral college and the latter by state legislatures), the appointment rather than election of judges, the life tenure of the judiciary, the veto power, and the power of judicial review (intended and implied but not actually spelled out in the Constitution)—not one of these institu-tional arrangements in the new government could be regarded as democratic. Only the House of Representatives was to be pop-ularly chosen. (Even for that body, the electorate would be re-stricted to those eligible to vote in state elections, and in some states this was still a relatively small part of the population.)

In addition, a number of restrictions on state powers, either by direct prohibition or through exclusive grants of power to the na-tional government, were intended to block the adoption by the states of measures likely to be demanded by popular majorities. States, for example, were denied the power to issue paper money, to legislate with regard to bankruptcy, or to "pass any . . . Law im-pairing the Obligation of Contracts." All of these powers might otherwise be employed (and in some states had already been em-ployed) to reduce the burden of debts owed by the agrarian ma-jority to the less numerous commercial group.

To the credit of its authors, the Constitution, while *non*democratic, was not thoroughly *anti*democratic. It did not establish democracy in the United States, but most of its provisions could be made compatible with democracy. The members of the Constitutional Convention were not eager to further the development of more popular government, but many could readily guess that it was likely to come. Very few shared Hamilton's unconcealed desire for monarchy or his highly unflattering view of the character of the public. The pattern of government for which they were responsible was flexible enough to be shifted readily to a democratic basis when occasion for it arose. Jefferson and other supporters of democracy recognized this fact. Working within the constitutional framework, the Jeffersonians and their Jacksonian successors managed, between 1790 and 1840, to make the American political system a basically democratic regime. The rise of political parties made a myth of the supposed independence of presidential electors and rendered the selection of the chief executive largely a matter of popular choice, and the abandonment of property qualifications for voting in almost all the states produced a practical result close to universal adult white male suffrage (extended by the Constitution to Negroes with the adoption of the Fourteenth and Fifteenth Amendments). The Senate's independence of direct popular control vanished in principle in 1913; in practice that independence had long been less than total.

Our judiciary is still nondemocratic, of course. Only when it plays a direct role in the making of governmental policy, as it does when it undertakes judicial review or the interpretation of key public laws, is this a matter of political concern. But judges study history, and the lessons of the Dred Scott decision in 1857 and of the anti-New Deal decisions of the 1930's are fairly obvious. In both instances, the prestige and authority lost by the judicial branch, and by the Supreme Court in particular, through the establishment of policies profoundly unpopular with most of the American people, were regained only with great difficulty over a considerable period of time. Life tenure and the absence of popular election have not rendered the courts totally free of popular influence.

In summary, there has been basic agreement in the United States as to the character of our political system for the last one hundred years, despite extremely serious earlier differences concerning that system. Our government is a republic, rather than a monarchy. It is federal, but our federalism makes the national government and its Constitution supreme and leaves the states sovereign only in the nostalgia of the unreconstructed. And it is democratic, being broadly based on the bulk of the adult population and subject to their ultimate control. To the extent that we maintain agreement on these features and develop no new disagreements over the character of our governmental system, our society possesses the first requisite of a healthy political system.

Agreement on Who Belongs to the System

In order for basic unity to be maintained in any country, a second requisite must also be present. This is agreement as to who belongs to the political system. Disagreement on this matter can take either of two forms. The first is insistence on the part of some group within the geographic area controlled by the society that it is not and does not wish to be part of that society. The corollary of this claim is usually a demand that the group be granted independence as a separate nation or that it be joined to another country to which its members feel stronger ties. The second form in which this problem can appear is the rejection by the rest of the society of a group which would very much like to be accepted as part of the society. Inescapably linked geographically (and therefore economically) to the people among whom they live, those belonging to such a group may discover that they are nevertheless rejected politically and socially. If such rejection continues over an extended period, it may even lead to demands for establishment of a separate political entity.

The first type of conflict has not been typical in the United States, although it is to be observed in many other countries. Much of Europe has long been troubled with national boundaries which do not (and sometimes cannot) coincide with ethnic, linguistic, and other social and cultural divisions. Consequently, from time to time many groups did not identify with the nation-states of which they were nominally parts. Much political friction, both international and domestic, has resulted. This problem is not confined to Europe, however. Tribal conflict in Central Africa, ethnic and religious differences in several Middle Eastern countries, and the position of the French-speaking inhabitants of Quebec are all examples of populations which do not regard themselves primarily as citizens of the nation in question, but whose loyalties in some cases are divided and in others lie altogether in different directions. Obviously, a society with such lack of identification is unstable. In the long run, it must gain the loyalty of the group in question, face the necessity of dividing its territory, or maintain a semblance of unity through force.

Although this situation in recent years has not been a serious problem for the United States, it has not been totally absent from our history. The Civil War came when one part of our population ceased to identify primarily with the nation and developed more significant loyalties to state and region. Initially by force and over a longer period through other devices, national unity was reestablished—a task made easier because until shortly before the Civil War very few Southerners had ceased to think of themselves as Americans and many did not do so even during the War.

We had to face the same problem when we acquired colonial possessions in other parts of the world, thereby establishing political authority over people who did not think of themselves as Americans, did not want to become Americans, and in some cases did not want to be ruled even temporarily by Americans. In the Philippine Islands a nasty guerrilla war (costing us as many casualties as the Spanish-American War) persisted for three years

27

after our nominal conquest of the islands from Spain. The Philippine situation was settled when the United States made a clearcut promise to grant independence within a limited period of time, a promise on which we made good. In Puerto Rico, where a large majority of the population has come to think of itself as American, this problem has not yet had to be faced in the same way. All in all, the absence of an extensive colonial empire and the fact that the areas in which we expanded on the North American continent were sparsely populated and could then be settled rather quickly by a large population migrating from the United States obviated the necessity of dealing in very many cases with a population subject to our control but profoundly unhappy about being part of the United States.

Already noted, however, is a second form in which this kind of problem can be found—the case of a group which *does* accept our society but which is rejected *by* that society. This problem we have had to face, and we are having to face it still. We had to face it even before the American Revolution occurred, when decisions were being made as to whether to impose religious restrictions on immigration and residence in the colonies. In several colonies this was done, penalties against Jews, Quakers, and Roman Catholics being particularly common. (All three of these groups, of course, were still subject to discrimination in England, from which most of the colonists had come.) The religious toleration for which several colonies (notably Pennsylvania, Rhode Island, and Maryland) were noted was not to be found in others. It is true that almost any group could find some colony in which it was welcome, and it is also true that in many colonies by the middle of the eighteenth century the prescribed penalties for theological deviation were being enforced with considerable laxity. Nevertheless, there had been enough religious persecution in an earlier time, especially in New England, to raise a real question as to whether the members of some religious groups were eligible to qualify as Americans. By 1791 a perhaps tentative but nonetheless official affirma-

28

tive answer had been given in the First Amendment. As far as the national government was concerned (and the same pattern was developing in most, though not all, of the states) the character of the individual's religion was to be irrelevant in connection with his relations with that government. "Membership" in America was not to be restricted on religious grounds.

Still other groups which might not have been admitted to full participation in our society were the successive waves of immigrants arriving from Europe throughout our history until the time of World War I. So long as those newcomers came from England, Scotland, and Northern Ireland, as had most of the inhabitants of the United States prior to the Revolution, there were relatively few objections, although one of these, the Alien Act of 1798, produced a great deal of political controversy before its repeal. A steady trickle of arrivals from other parts of Europe was already to be seen, however, and occasional complaints against the entry of Germans into Pennsylvania and the French into New England had been voiced.

With the 1840's a major change occurred in the sources of immigration. A few continued to come from England and Scotland, but a veritable transatlantic tide surged in from Ireland and Germany, produced in the former country by the potato famine and in the latter by religious friction and by the political turmoil surrounding the Revolution of 1848. For three reasons these newcomers met resistance on a scale completely outside the experience of earlier arrivals. First, the obvious and immediate need for large numbers of people from external sources to help to populate a sparsely settled country was beginning to pass. The coastal area, and for that matter almost the entire region east of the Mississippi, had been settled by the middle of the nineteenth century. Although abundant land was still available farther west, most of the Irish and many of the Germans had no wish to play pioneer in a region whose nature was almost totally unfamiliar to them. Instead, they remained in Eastern cities—many of them in the ports where they

29

had landed. Despite the rapidly growing industry of this area, jobs were not always easy to find, and where they became available it was often because higher-paid native labor had been displaced to make them available. It is scarcely surprising that as a consequence a political movement appeared with the twin goals of preventing future immigration and of restricting the political, social, and economic influence of those who had already been admitted. We will discuss this movement in the next chapter, but we should note here that two other factors added to the antagonism against Germans and Irish.

For the former, language was a barrier. Never before had this country received such a large body of immigrants whose past contact with the Anglo-Saxon part of the world was so limited that even elementary communication was a problem. The Irish occasioned very little trouble of linguistic origin, but religion created a problem of equal significance, and it was one which also applied to many, though not all, of the Germans. With few exceptions, the English and Irish Catholics who originally settled Maryland being the only important examples, citizens of the United States had been Protestants until the appearance of the Irish and Germans. The earlier religious disputes among competing Protestant denominations had been difficult enough to keep within bounds. Now an even more basic religious division was involved—a division which Great Britain had been unable to bridge at the political level during the three previous centuries and a division with the reconciliation of which this country had had little experience.

Several decades were required before something approximating genuine political assimilation of the Irish could be accomplished. (Some may suggest that the *conclusive* indication that this had been successfully done did not come until the election of John F. Kennedy as President in 1960.) For the Germans, full political acceptance came somewhat earlier, especially in such Middle Western states as Missouri and Wisconsin, but even there it was not achieved overnight. It should be emphasized that the conflicts which centered around the Irish and the Germans were due to no rejection by these groups of the country in which they found themselves. They had come to the United States voluntarily. They had come for a wide variety of reasons, many of which had little to do with politics, but they did not bring with them any antagonism toward our political system. There were certainly some cultural and social differences between them and the Americans who had arrived here earlier, and some of those differences were bound to create problems of various sorts. But at the political level the problems were created primarily by those who had been Americans before them. The Irish and German immigrants wanted to be Americans too, and for many years they found that those who arrived here first refused to accept them as such. Lessons had to be learned on both sides, but the most difficult to absorb was the lesson that those with religious and cultural backgrounds which differed from those of earlier Americans could be Americans too, that those whose accents carried traces of languages which were not English could be Americans too, and that those whose names were spelled in ways unfamiliar to an earlier generation of Americans could be Americans too.

When we had scarcely begun to face up to the necessity of finding ways to accept the Irish and the Germans politically we were forced to deal also with large numbers of immigrants from countries even further removed from us socially and culturally. Within a quarter of a century after the end of the Civil War, a large majority of newly arriving immigrants were coming from such places as Poland, Russia, Scandinavia, Hungary, Bohemia, Italy, and Greece. To each the same resistance developed; for each the same slow process of gaining acceptance as Americans was necessary. For each this process was in the end at least partially successful, although the same factors of language, religion, and economic competition made the process difficult.

All of these groups, however, had one distinct advantage in the process of becoming accepted as Americans. They did, after all, *look* like Americans. True, there were characteristics of features or complexion or hair coloring by which one was supposed to be able to recognize a Swede or an Italian or a Jew, but these were far from dependable in practice. In fact, once the immigrant had acquired American clothing, had begun to patronize American barber shops, had smoothed the rough edges off his accent, and had developed a flair for idomatic American English (which might require a new generation and some public schooling), it became extremely difficult and often quite impossible for a stranger to tell whether the new American or his father came originally from Liverpool, Cork, Prague, or Indianapolis, unless he chose to divulge the information. This became even more true if he decided to abandon the neighborhood and the social and religious ties which bound him to those who shared the same ethnic and linguistic background.

For others, however, this was not true. The Chinese or Japanese carried his ethnic identification badge on his face. So did the American Indian and some Mexicans. So, above all, did the Negro. It is at least in part for that reason that the ethnic group which has had the most difficult time gaining full political acceptance in the United States has been the non-British group which has been here in large numbers for the longest time. The first slaves from Africa arrived in Virginia as early as 1619, and all of those legally imported had arrived by 1808, when Congress prohibited the slave trade (although some continued to be brought in illegally for more than a half century thereafter). Yet almost three and a half centuries after the first Negro slaves came to America, some Americans have still not decided whether those slaves' descendants are really Americans or not, and if they are, to what extent. Our relative success in gaining acceptance for Americans coming from dozens of nations has not been matched in this case. The main reason for this is the obvious element of color, rendering the Negro recognizable as such no matter what he accomplishes in other respects. A contributing factor, especially in the South, was the historical factor of slavery itself, a factor which neither the Negro nor the white could ever quite forget.

Like the immigrants from Europe, the Negro did not create the clash with the longer-established Americans. It is true that he had come unwillingly to America. But once he was here, there was nothing he could be but an American. African cultures were lost within a generation or two on this side of the Atlantic. In America the Negro's language became English; his religion became Christianity, and the rest of his culture was also provided by his owner and by the country of which he was now part. That culture sometimes underwent considerable modification in the process of being handed down, but little or nothing African remained in it—little or nothing that could not be traced to American sources. Even the most distinctive attribute of Negro life—music—was American Negro music, not African music. The only thing to which the Negro could aspire politically and socially was full acceptance in this society. He had no real alternative. And yet this acceptance was what he could not gain. He had no wish to destroy our society or to create a separate one of his own. Neither was possible if he had wanted it. But neither, apparently, was it possible for him to become a full-fledged member of American society.

At first it was slavery through which we indicated that the Negro was not an American and scarcely even a human. The occasional practice of manumission began to produce a considerable group of free Negroes, but these too were surrounded, especially in the South after 1830, by so many restrictions as to make it clear that they were not regarded as full participants in this nation. Even in the North, where slavery had been eliminated many decades earlier, Negroes as late as 1860 were permitted to vote in only a handful of states. The most striking demonstration of the refusal to admit Negroes under any circumstances to the privileges of Americanism came in the Dred Scott decision in 1857. Chief Justice Taney, speaking for the Supreme Court of the United States, insisted that Negroes had not been treated as citizens at the time of the adoption of the Constitution and therefore could not come to be regarded as citizens within the meaning of the Constitution at any later time, whether slave or free. This most formal of denials of membership in our society was subsequently reversed by the Fourteenth Amendment, and never since then has there been an official insistence at the national level that Negroes cannot be Americans. On the contrary, being an American, from the standpoint of citizenship, is defined quite specifically so as to include not only Negroes but other groups within our boundaries about whom any serious question might be raised:

> All persons born or naturalized in the United States, and subject to the jurisdiction thereof, are citizens of the United States and of the States wherein they reside.

Formal citizenship is not, of course, necessarily to be equated with complete political acceptance. Almost a century has gone by since the ratification of the Fourteenth Amendment, but the Negro's citizenship over much of that time has been little more than nominal. Even voting itself, the most limited act which we can call really political, has often been denied to Negroes, in spite of the clear wording of the Fourteenth and Fifteenth Amendments. Even today it remains extremely difficult or impossible for a Negro to vote in many parts of the Deep South, although elsewhere old obstacles barring the way to the suffrage have become much easier to surmount. But in many other ways—political, legal, social, and economic—Negroes continue to be made aware that to much of the white segment of the population they are not really Americans. Only extraordinarily intense efforts by both Negroes and those whites who believe in helping to secure for them all the rights of Americans have gained even the very limited advances with which they have so far had to content themselves.

One real danger in this situation is that Negroes may begin to reject the society which rejects them. Plentiful signs indicate that for a small minority of that race this has already happened, although a substantial majority of Negroes and of their leaders continue to assume that their future is a future as Americans. For those who have ceased to believe this, two possible courses are open. No longer identifying themselves as Americans, they may commence agitation for separation from the society of which they do not believe they can be a part. It is this which distinguishes the approach of the Black Muslim movement. Concluding that white Americans do not want them, they have decided that they want no part of a White America. Treated as an alien force within the country, they have resolved really to become an alien force. Regarded as a hostile element, they have become one. No longer seeking to become Americans, they regard the America they know as the enemy. In practical terms, there is no realistic way in which they can achieve the goal of separation that they profess, but if their numbers should increase substantially, they could, in the process of seeking that goal, make life much less pleasant for other members of their race and for the rest of the country.

There is a second direction in which Negroes who give up on American society might move. Recognizing that it is impossible for them to live apart from the society to which they are geographically and economically tied, they could join the ranks of those who denounce the fundamental character of that society and who wish to destroy the basic political and social institutions of that society and to replace them with arrangements of an entirely new design. Most of the groups of the extreme right have been closed to Negroes. The left, however, is another matter, and the failure of the Communist Party to gain greater support among American Negroes must be attributed both to good luck and to a considerable fund of political common sense among Negroes and their leaders. Many of them have had little enough reason to support the American political system, given the way it has operated in relation to them, and only their confidence that in the future that system would be in part theirs can account for their behavior. Propagandists for democracy can point to the existence of that confidence, right here in this country, as one of their more striking successes.

The United States has managed to assimilate politically an impressively broad range of people from widely varying backgrounds. It has done so in some cases in an astonishingly short period of time, and it can take genuine pride in having found this possible at all. Few other countries have gone as far as we have in attempting to divorce the concept of membership in the society from the concept of national origin. Here we are all immigrants or the offspring of immigrants—many of us fairly recent immigrants —and being more or less aware of that fact we tend to be ready to accept someone as an American whether his parents were or not. But our relative success should not hide from us the distance we remain from the full accomplishment of the goal of making all who live here Americans. Until we are truly ready to accept the Negro, Puerto Rican, Mexican-American, and Oriental as Americans like us, we should not spend too much time congratulating ourselves on having taken, after a century and a quarter of declining to do so, the relatively small step of admitting to the Presidency an American of Irish ancestry and Catholic religion.

Agreement Not *Necessary on Specific Policies*

Although fundamental agreement on the basic character of the political system and on who is to be accepted as belonging to that system is essentially important, disagreement is permissible in some areas of the healthy political system. There are few who would demand absolute and total conformity in all things under any government. In a democracy it is particularly important to retain as much scope as possible for differences among individuals and groups, for the freedom to be different from one's fellows is one of the great advantages of democracy. In principle, there is seldom very much quarrel over this rule. The problem comes in trying to decide which policies are fundamental to the basic character of the political system and which, although perhaps important enough in themselves, can be altered without destroying any of the essential elements of the system itself.

To some Americans, for example, religion is central to their concept of Americanism. Many go further and add that not just any religion will do, for to them America is above all a Christian nation. Some go further and restrict the Christianity in question to Protestant (or, as the case may be, Catholic) Christianity. To these people, the correct and appropriate purpose of government is the furtherance of true religion and of the sort of life which is compatible with their version of that religion. To these people, therefore, any issue which touches on matters of religious principle becomes an issue fundamental to the character of the political system. Moral questions always take on that character, which is one reason why intelligent politicians try so hard to avoid having to deal with issues which have religious or moral aspects. The standard rules of politics, which are pragmatic and fairly rational, simply do not apply in such cases, for such issues are always likely to explode in totally unexpected directions.

For the most part, Americans have successfully ducked these questions. The central focus of our politics has usually been economics, and on the occasions when moral issues have occupied the center of our political stage they have tended not to stay there very long. Slavery was such an issue, but for the majority on both sides it was the most crucial question for only a rather limited period. For Lincoln, as for most Northerners, the Civil War became a crusade against slavery only well after the beginning of the war. Prohibition was another religious and moral proposition, but enthusiasm for it survived in most Americans for little more than a decade. Other such questions come along from time to time, but most attract widespread attention for only a short while.

An explanation for the failure of religion to intrude into American politics is not difficult to find. Most of the American people simply are not as religious as their widespread church membership and attendance would suggest. Their commitment to religion is more a social gesture than a basic governing element in their lives. This is not to cast doubt on the sincerity with which those religious views are held but simply to suggest that it does not occur to most Americans that all of their individual and social decisions ought to be made on the basis of theological principles. Outside such areas as sexual mores, their implied response to religious criticism of their behavior is, "What has religion got to do with this?" Whatever its consequences from the standpoint of the theologian or the moralist, this attitude is responsible for a major part of the consensus which exists within the American governmental system.

Religion is not the only topic which can produce highly dogmatic attitudes. Another area in which some people insist that certain policies must be equated with the survival of the political system itself is foreign policy. To at least a limited degree, they are correct. Obviously enough, total failure in the area of foreign policy is bound to lead to the destruction of the society. The minimal goals of any country in international relations are the maintenance of its national independence and its territorial integrity. In practice, most countries will wish to accomplish even more in foreign affairs. But to assume that these goals can be accomplished only with one particular set of policies and that all other approaches to the problem therefore constitute treachery is much more doubtful, and it becomes still more doubtful when it is also insisted that the correct policy is immutable and will always remain correct, no matter what the circumstances. In foreign relations, as in other fields, the achievement even of constant goals is likely to demand considerable flexibility as to specific measures.

The most common area in which we find claims that particular policies are essential to the basic nature of our constitutional system is economics. Often in political debate and occasionally in more official statements, including more than one historic decision of the Supreme Court in an earlier time, we find Americans insisting that a particular economic program is essential to our survival as a free society or that another would destroy our country as we have known it. There is certainly a relationship between political and economic institutions, and the nature of the one is often influenced by the character of the other. Yet this relationship is seldom as simple as the loudest of spokesmen for a variety of economic viewpoints would pretend, and a particular political arrangement may be compatible with a variety (though not an infinite variety) of economic policies.

The most common argument along this line in the contemporary United States is the insistence that the American political system is inseparable from the economic pattern of "free enterprise"—a term which still lacks an adequate definition but which seems to mean something close to what was traditionally called capitalism. It cannot be denied that American democracy grew up side by side with an American economy subject largely to private control (albeit private control for the most part through relatively large corporations). However, it is far from demonstrated that this is the *only* economic pattern which would permit the survival of the American political system as we have known it. Since few academicians and politicians and almost no businessmen in this country have been willing to push the doctrine of laissez faire to its ultimate limits, we have always had a substantial amount of governmental activity on the American economic scene, and there have been from time to time great variations in the extent and nature of that activity. Our political system has survived those changes without being itself changed in any revolutionary way as a result, and it can no doubt survive a great many more. Indeed, one of the great assets of our system is that it is flexible enough to permit some experimentation, in economics as in other things; to accomplish the ends we think desirable, we can alter specific policies and programs as often as we find necessary.

There are, however, some extremes in the economic realm which probably cannot be reconciled with democratic government. One is the extreme of severe economic privation involving a large part of the population of the country over an extended period of time. The poverty of a small minority need not affect the rest of the system, although it is certainly to be deplored on other grounds. Economic distress among a majority or an extremely large minority is another matter. The political unrest which is likely to result jeopardizes the stability of the system. Aside from that, democracy demands of the general population some effort to assess their political decisions in terms of their own long-range needs and desires; if all their energies are absorbed in a struggle merely to keep themselves and their families alive for another day, this sort of semirational political action will be out of the question.

Although there may be some legitimate argument about this proposition, it is also doubtful that democracy is compatible with complete governmental control of *all* property and *all* types of economic activity. Where the possibility of gaining any kind of employment and of supporting one's family is subject to the approval of administrative authorities, the prospect of free political action is obviously limited. However, it should be made clear that this applies only in the case of total or very nearly total governmental control, not to the situation in which certain types of economic activity are subjected to governmental regulation but others are left largely independent. As the recent experience of the United States, Great Britain, Canada, Australia, and most of Western Europe makes obvious, political freedom can survive and opposition political activity can continue even though extensive economic activities are undertaken directly by the government and others are required to operate under governmental regulation. So long as a sphere remains for private economic activity and so long as the pattern of government regulation of the economy continues to be subject to ultimate public control through the political process, democracy can survive.

The most dogmatic apologists for "free enterprise" are mistaken in their view that liberty is possible only in an environment of complete laissez faire, minimal taxation, and the absence of government ownership of property and regulation of business activity. But so, of course, are the dogmatic Marxists, with their insistence that liberty can be meaningful only if all the means of production and distribution are in public hands or subject to direct and complete public control. Whether democracy can survive in either of these extreme situations is open to question, but it is absurd to argue that it can survive *only* with total government or with total absence of such control. The real answer is that political freedom can be accompanied by any of a wide variety of economic systems. Only the extremes are excluded—the extreme of total governmental control of all economic activity, the extreme of utterly selfish and irresponsible private control, and the extreme of widespread poverty and privation.

Other Symptoms of Political Breakdown

Three indicators of basic political ills have been noted: disagreement as to the fundamental character of the political system, denial of membership to significant groups within the society or refusal by those groups to operate as part of the society, and insistence by part of the population that only if certain policies are followed will they regard the government as legitimate. There are, however, other symptoms which may suggest that a dangerous situation exists. One of them is the disappearance of organized political opposition. A powerful political organization or machine is not necessarily dangerous in itself; indeed, it can make government work more efficiently and more responsibly. But when there is no opposition to provide criticism of the party or machine in power and to provide an alternative crew of governmental leaders and alternative policies, a fundamental element of democracy disappears. The failure to hold fair and honest elections is one way in which opposition may be rendered ineffective, but the situation may be equally dangerous when the organized opposition does not perform satisfactorily even though there is honest and free balloting.

41

To be contrasted with the situation in which the opposition fails to perform its task properly is the government which fails to govern. There is bound to be disagreement as to precisely what the society expects its government to do, but only a very few people, the anarchists, can honestly say that they want government to do *nothing.* In a complex society, however, a multiplicity of parties or a multiplicity of factions and interests within one or two parties may produce essentially negative results. This tendency may be enlarged by institutional and procedural arrangements which make it extremely difficult to produce new or changed governmental policies. The American tendency to emphasize the limitation and control of political power, which has been under some circumstances a very healthy tendency, has sometimes caused us to lose sight of the necessity of making sure that our government has adequate power and authority to do what we want it to do. When it does not, general frustration is bound to result, and this must lead to instability and to a possible repudiation of democratic government itself in favor of systems which give promise of being able to act more forcefully, more quickly, and more effectively.

Closely tied to the previous problem is the phenomenon which political scientists and social psychologists have come to call "political alienation." Under some circumstances, citizens may lose the conviction that their government has very much to do with them. If many of them become convinced that their political actions, including voting, participation in party work and in campaigns, and interest-group activities, have no impact on the course of political events and that they have no real control over what their government does, such alienation is present. This can easily happen when people begin to believe that there are no real differences between political parties and among political leaders and that election results will make no real difference in terms of the actual policies pursued by government. Such a situation can lead to nonvoting or to irrational and inconsistent voting. It can lead also to a rejection of democracy itself.

3. Historical Failures of American Consensus

$\mathcal{T}$he previous chapter presented some of the fundamental requisites of a healthy political system, including two
which are particularly crucial—general agreement (or consensus)
as to the basic character of that system and similar agreement as
to who belongs to the system. Noted also were a number of examples of lack of consensus—some which have vanished with
history and some which are still with us. The five failures of
American consensus to be analyzed in this chapter fall into a
special category. In one sense each belongs to the past, having appeared on the American scene and then disappeared. Each, however, has left us a legacy of division and distrust from which we
have not been able fully to escape. And each illustrates a problem
which may recur from time to time in the future.

The Civil War

No episode in American history—neither the Ameri-
can Revolution itself nor the tremendous changes in American life
during the twentieth century—has had quite the significance of the
Civil War. No other has left such obvious marks upon our society
such a long time after the event. No other illustrates in such a

fundamental way the consequences of a basic lack of consensus, for on no other occasion was the framework of our constitutional system of government actually ruptured. Even today, one hundred years later, a great deal of time and effort is constantly being spent in an effort to deal with the same problems with which that war was concerned and with others which were created at least in part by that struggle.

The implication of the Southern position on the national-state relationship was that the states were sovereign political entities bound in a tie with other states and with the nation which was only as strong as each state found it advantageous to make it. The logic of nullification and interposition was the logic of the Articles of Confederation. Carried to its limits, it meant that the Constitution, which had been written and adopted for the purpose of strengthening those features of national power which had been found dangerously weak under the Articles, represented no substantial changes from the pattern under those Articles. When extended to the point of secession, it meant a reduction from even the negligible unity present under the Articles, whose full title was, after all, the Articles of Confederation and *Perpetual* Union. If the Southern position was correct, the Constitution amounted to nothing more than a loose working relationship among the states— a relationship which each state was free to interpret for itself in every case where a conflict might develop and a relationship which each state was free to terminate on any occasion which seemed to it a satisfactory excuse for doing so. Their failure to end the union prior to 1860 was due to no legal or political inhibition, according to this argument, but solely to there having been no occasion of conflict serious enough to warrant the dissolution of an otherwise advantageous tie. To Calhoun and his Southern associates and successors, the United States was not truly a nation but only a confederation or alliance.

Nationalism was a more potent force than had been assumed by Southern political leaders, however. It was the one issue through which Lincoln could forge and maintain a unity of will and purpose which would sustain the North through four years of the bloodiest war this country has ever fought and sustain it until victory had been achieved. Furthermore, national loyalty even in the South was great enough to prevent the secession of four of the slave states (Delaware, Kentucky, Maryland, and Missouri), great enough to cause a schism in a fifth (Virginia, a significant part of which rejoined the Union as West Virginia), great enough to cause a substantial number of Southerners to fight on the Union side (including such notable figures as General George Thomas and Admiral David Porter), and great enough to produce a conspicuous lack of enthusiasm among some who gave their nominal allegiance to the Confederacy. In addition, the South was to discover that fighting a war for the principle of states' rights was to fight on a self-defeating basis. A war machine in which the drafting of troops, the supply of revenue through taxation, and even the movement of military units are subject to the control of the individual state authorities is bound to be quite inefficient. Yet that is precisely the sort of military and political organization which Jefferson Davis and Robert E. Lee had to try to run. (The Southern devotion to states' rights during the Civil War illustrates one of the great dangers of political propaganda—those who employ it may eventually come to believe it!)

All of this would be merely an interesting historical exercise, if the slogans of the spokesmen for disunity before and during the Civil War did not make annoying and sometimes dangerous reappearances in our own time. Within the last decade, for the first time in a century, we have heard talk again of interposition, if not of nullification and secession. In some Southern states interposition during the 1950's amounted to the passage of a legislative resolution of defiance and nothing more, but in others state authorities took more concrete steps to hinder the enforcement by national authorities of decisions legally made through the political institutions of this nation. As during the period before the Civil War, the claim has been made that a "sovereign" state is not required to comply with those features of national policy which it finds contrary to the fundamental views of significant parts of its own population. Usually this argument is presented as part of a protest against judicial decisions involving race relations and is accompanied by a claim that those decisions are themselves in violation of the Constitution. Yet this argument can be upheld only if it is assumed that the final word as to interpretation of any provision of the Constitution which is controversial rests with the individual states, rather than with the national courts. This doctrine is contrary to the Supremacy Clause of the Constitution and to a long line of judicial decisions beginning as early as 1810. It is also incompatible with the concept of nationhood itself.

The numerous attempts to bolster the state sovereignty argument by reference to the Tenth Amendment are equally faulty. That amendment reads:

The powers not delegated to the United States by the Constitution, nor prohibited by it to the States, are reserved to the States respectively, or to the people.

No one quarrels with this statement, which is clearly implied by the wording of the Constitution, even without this amendment. Nothing in this amendment gives to the individual states the authority to determine *which* powers have been so delegated. On the contrary, the journals of the Constitutional Convention, Hamilton's words in No. 78 of *The Federalist,* and a line of judicial decisions including both Marbury *v.* Madison and McCulloch *v.* Maryland support the assumption that this decision can be made only at the national level. Even more reprehensible is the attempt of some Southern politicians to improve their position by misquoting this amendment in public utterances and inserting an extra word and reading, "The powers not *expressly* delegated . . ." The argument against implied powers was disposed of by John Marshall in Mc-

Culloch *v.* Maryland 145 years ago with an effectiveness which should require no reiteration today.

For those to whom the Civil War provides no convincing historical evidence of the end of state sovereignty, there are plenty of additional indications of its impracticability in the latter part of the twentieth century. In an age of universal international insecurity, foreign policy and national defense are difficult enough to implement with a unified nation supporting them; they are impossible to direct successfully if doubts are continually raised as to the extent to which any given part of the country will support them. The economic well-being of the United States and our attempts to increase our economic strength are dependent on the continuing performance of this country as a single economic system. The size of this economic unit accounts in large part for our impressive economic accomplishments—a lesson not lost on those in other parts of the world, such as the countries of the European Common Market.

Perhaps the most important reason for rejecting the states'-rights approach is the fact that most Americans have long since decided to give their primary loyalties to their nation, rather than to any of its component units. Unanimity in this respect does not yet exist. A significant minority still think of themselves primarily in terms of a particular state; for a smaller group their cities play the same role. Possibly an eccentric soul somewhere considers even his county or his sewer-and-garbage-removal district most important. Most of us, however, identify ourselves above all as Americans, and the rest of our political ties command only a lesser emotional loyalty. Adding to this national solidarity is the extraordinary geographic mobility of modern Americans. For many, residence in one community or even one region for more than three or four years at a time is unusual. Census data suggest that the time is almost here when the average American dies in some state other than the one in which he was born. The typical American of an earlier day had been born, raised, and educated—and expected to live, die, and be buried—within a relatively tiny geographic area, which might easily under those circumstances become a focus for his affection. The American who was never in a given community until last year and who does not expect ever to be there again after next year does not react in the same way. He is likely to identify with his business or profession or with the firm which employs him or with his labor union or other economic or social organization or with his church or his political party. In terms of governmental units he identifies with his nation.

The other legacy of the Civil War is, of course, the conflict over the place of the Negro in our society. We have never really settled it, although the precise character of the controversy has changed a great deal over the years—sometimes slowly and sometimes with dramatic speed. Yet the heart of the problem has remained the same. Is the Negro a person? If he is, should he occupy the same political position as other persons? If he should not, in what respects is it proper to treat him differently? If, for political purposes, he ought to be the same as other people, how may we best assure him of such treatment?

All that the Civil War definitely settled about the Negro was that he was no longer to be a slave and that he was, from the legal standpoint, entitled to the privileges of citizenship, including the right to vote. The last two points, incidentally, are still challenged by some Southern spokesmen, who insist that the Fourteenth and Fifteenth Amendments were never validly made parts of the Constitution. Their argument is dubious legally and absurd politically, for ninety-five years of general acceptance have made these amendments as much a part of the American political system as any other principles we profess. (We can perhaps be thankful that few, if any, of our contemporary racists have attempted to deny the validity of the Thirteenth Amendment as well and to present an argument for the re-establishment of slavery.) Beyond the abolition of slavery, which was undeniably of extreme importance, and the grants of citizenship and suffrage, which might or might not be important, depending on how they were interpreted and implemented, many questions demanded answers. During the last century significant changes in those answers have developed.

Both the Southern effort to replace slavery with something approximating serfdom, through the so-called Black Codes, and the Radical Republican effort to impose a political system by which Negroes and those whites allied with them could permanently dominate the South, through Reconstruction, failed. The first failed because political power in 1865 lay almost entirely with the North, and the second failed because a majority of Northerners lost what little zeal they had ever possessed for making the war anything more than an effort to restore the Union. For most of them the problem of the Negro defied solution and in any case, was irrelevant to their concerns, which, as always, were primarily economic in nature. The end of Reconstruction did not provide an absolute answer to questions concerning the status of the Negro, however. Not until fifteen years later did the pattern of rigid racial segregation appear in the South, accompanied by denial to Southern Negroes of any effective right to vote.

With the Civil War began also the movement of Negroes from the rural South to Southern and then Northern cities, a movement which has drastically changed the nature of the race problem in recent decades. Denied in the South, after 1890, the full citizenship promised him in the 1860's, the Negro discovered that this citizenship, in an imperfect fashion, was available to him in the North. Eventually it was to confer upon him some limited political power in that part of the United States—power which he could then use to promote still further improvements in his condition, both North and South.

In the end, then, the Civil War left us with a restored Union but only a partially restored consensus, and it left us with some problems which were to require a long time for solution—more time in some cases than we have yet had. It left us free of the later threat of secession and with a general commitment to the principle of national supremacy—a commitment which was to have no more than grudging acceptance in most of the South, however, and which was to be denied later by a minority even outside the South. It left us committed as a nation to the theoretical proposition that the Negro was a human being and, for some purposes at least, ought to be treated like any other human being. But most Southerners and many Northerners remained dubious of the first proposition and frankly hostile to any very generous interpretation of the second. It is only the Civil War, of all our political struggles of previous centuries, from which we retain such major unresolved problems today.

Nativism

The American nativist movement has actually popped up on several different occasions during our history, and echoes of it recur from time to time even now. Its most vigorous outburst, in the early 1850's, antedated the Civil War, and political groupings based on distrust of immigrants and aliens can be traced back to the Alien Act of 1798 and even to the pre-Revolutionary period. It was antagonism to the Irish who had arrived here in the 1840's, however, which presented this problem in its most serious form. For the only time in our history a political party was organized around this single issue.

The Know-Nothings, or the American Party, as they were formally styled, had several reasons for their antagonism toward the Irish. One was simple religious bigotry. The small Catholic groups in Maryland and elsewhere had appeared to pose no serious threat to the predominantly Protestant character of the United States, but the wave of Irish was another matter. In terms of sheer numbers, if nothing else, they altered the situation, assuming the mass of arrivals was to continue. Of course, it could not continue, if for no other reason than that soon no one would be left in Ireland. But

"No popery!" was an old cry in the politics of the English-speaking world, and for a brief time it competed with slavery as the stuff of American politics just before the Civil War.

Probably as important as the religious question was the matter of economic competition. Just beginning to achieve a significant improvement in their standard of living, partly because of the general economic growth of the country and partly because of the successes of the first rudimentary efforts at labor-union organization, native-born employees were threatened because the new immigrants, often in desperate economic circumstances when they arrived, had no choice but to accept jobs at whatever wages were offered and to live at an economic level substantially below that to which Americans were becoming accustomed. This, in turn, led to reduced wages and unemployment among the native-born workers, particularly during the periodic economic crises and depressions which were becoming characteristic of this country.

The most impressive political performance by the Know-Nothings was in the state elections of 1854, but the political strength gained then was dissipated through ridiculous investigations of the supposedly subversive Catholic schools and of the allegedly widespread kidnapping of girls into convents. By 1856 this sort of nonsense, plus the increased tension over slavery, had deprived the party of its audience, who had more important things to worry about. Its Presidential candidate, former President Millard Fillmore, carried but a single state, his party's Northern wing having already tied itself to the newly emerging Republican Party.

In a very real sense, of course, Know-Nothingism had nothing really to offer to American society, although its origin lay in concern over two quite serious questions—the living standards of working people and their families and the assimilation of large numbers of newcomers to this country—as well as a variety of thoroughly specious issues. Both of the real questions were to require eventual action, but the sheer hostility to "foreigners" voiced

51

by the nativists could not be the answer. Already in the middle of an unprecedented geographic and economic expansion, we needed as much of a labor force as we could find. Halting immigration at that time would have been absurd. The United States, already engaged in a bitter struggle over whether the Negro could be also an American, could not afford the effort to set up in addition a second and permanently inferior category of whites, based on the geographic location of their births, denying to those from abroad citizenship and its corresponding political and social rights and responsibilities. Americans may not have been sure how far they wanted to carry the notion of democracy, but there were few indeed, either in the North and West or in the Southern states from Alabama on west, who supported the European pattern of rigid social classes with few political or social ties among them and little potential mobility across class lines.

Instead of rejecting the immigrants or condemning them to a permanent second-class status, we simply made them Americans. This task could not be accomplished overnight, and it was accompanied by a great deal of struggle, disappointment, and heartache. Intense feeling continued to surround the Irish in most Eastern cities through the rest of the nineteenth century. Germans, to a lesser extent, and at a later time Italians, Jews, Swedes, Poles, Hungarians, Czechs, Greeks, and others faced the same problem. But in the end they all became Americans. They joined our society and they accepted our culture, modifying both in the process but, in essential respects leaving them American. Political hostility to these groups gradually died away as this happened, and so did social antagonism, except where it was reinforced by religious prejudice or by conflict with the urban social milieu and its economic interests, for the descendants of most of the immigrants did remain in or near the cities. But most of the rest of the American population was moving there too, so that even this made less and less difference as time went on.

Efforts to rally Americans to battle to restore the Anglo-Saxon* character of our institutions still occupy a great deal of the time of some "patriotic" organizations and are of significant political value in some parts of the country. Nationally, they get nowhere, nor should they, for our political institutions have survived and will continue to survive both the immigrants and the anti-immigrants. In terms of those institutions we are still an Anglo-Saxon society, for it was from British origins that we borrowed most of those we did not invent ourselves. Many American cultural attributes, of which our language is only the most obvious, must be traced to the same source. And all of this is not in the slightest degree less true since the part of our population whose ancestors came from England, Scotland, and Northern Ireland ceased to be a majority of that population.

The Ku Klux Klan

The original Ku Klux Klan, which flourished during the period of Reconstruction in the South, is of little concern to us here. Part of the Southern reaction to specific aspects of that phase of American history, it came to an end, for practical purposes, as soon as that episode ended, and it had little or nothing in common with twentieth-century organizations of the same name. The most powerful of the later groups, appearing about the time of the First World War, achieved such power during the early 1920's that it threatened to gain complete control of several state govern-

---

* American usage of this term varies but seems to have little to do with any strict linguistic or ethnic distinctions. The Scotch and Scotch-Irish have always been included, to the horror of any Scot who takes seriously his nation's ancient conflict with the English. So, often enough, are Americans of German, Dutch, and Swiss background. "Anglo-Saxon" seems to have come to apply to any white American who is a Protestant and whose ancestors seem to have lived at some time north of the Alps and west of the Vistula. Those of English or Scottish background qualify even if Catholic.

ments and to accomplish the disintegration of the Democratic Party. Nor was the Klan of the 1920's confined to the South, although it was certainly active there. Its greatest strength actually lay in the Middle West and Southwest, with the Pacific Coast challenging the Deep South for third place; even in the state of New York it is estimated to have had as many as 200,000 members.

Of all the organizations in American history which have been built around hatred, the Klan was probably the most indiscriminate in its bigotry. On one ground or another it hated very nearly everything and everybody: Negroes, Catholics, Jews, Chinese, Japanese, aliens and naturalized citizens of all varieties, religious modernists, bootleggers and their customers, and those transgressing the strictest code of ethics in the area of sex. Some of its members certainly did not share its zealous concern on the last two counts, but almost anyone with a mind to do some hating could find an appropriate target somewhere in the above list and could become a good Klansman if he were so inclined, unless, of course, he himself belonged to one of the despised categories. In that case, he would have to do his hating on an unorganized basis.

What the Klan was really reacting against was the transformation of the United States along several lines, with some of which the particular groups it was fighting had very little to do. Above all, Klan members were distressed by the modern urban and industrialized society in which they found themselves living. It was not the sort of society to which they could easily adjust. They had grown up in what they thought was a rural, unsophisticated, white, Anglo-Saxon, and Protestant America. But the America of farms and small towns had come to be dominated by great cities and was seemingly threatening to vanish altogether. Protestants were still a majority but a much smaller majority, and those who were both white and Anglo-Saxon had come to be only a minority, except in rural areas, although their political, social, and economic influence remained extraordinarily great. Most serious of all, perhaps, was the newly developing American culture, which was identified, with considerable accuracy, with the cities. It was thoroughly American, and yet it was not the old American culture. It was more sophisticated and more complex, and it was subject to a wider variety of influences. In many fields—religion, education, entertainment, marriage and divorce, sex, drinking and smoking, and technology —it conflicted with the standards of those who identified with the older America. It simply was not their America; yet they had to live in it. To seek someone to blame for such a predicament is perhaps natural, and the ethnic, religious, and social groups which had seemed absent from the old rural society were an obvious choice.

Catholics, Jews, and Negroes had in fact had very little to do with causing these changes. They tended to settle in cities because that is where jobs were most readily available when they arrived in the United States or when they left the Deep South—testimony to the extent to which urban growth and industrial development were already taking place. If any group had to be selected for blame, it should logically have been the "captains of industry," whose financial and entrepreneurial skills had played such an important role in the fantastically rapid growth of manufacturing and commerce during the nineteenth century. From that development came the urbanization and all the important social and cultural changes it was to produce. But no one group deserves the credit or the blame for all of this. In a very real sense it was implicit in the American situation and probably could not have been avoided under any circumstances, even if we had truly wanted to avoid it. It was well under way fairly early in the nineteenth century, and it is difficult to conceive of anything which could have stopped or reversed it by the time of the Civil War.

What is obvious to us was by no means so apparent however, to the Klan members in the 1920's. Most of them knew little of history and nothing of social science, but they did know what they disliked, and their efforts to eradicate the things they disliked threatened for a brief time to disrupt the entire political structure of the country. Their hopeless battle against the history of modern

America died away when the groups they were attacking organized for political action on the other side, when established political leaders became wary of pawning their political careers to an organization most of whose demands were impossible of realization, and when, eventually, the depression gave everyone something more important to worry about. The seeming revivals of the KKK since World War II have produced in most of the country only a pale imitation of the mighty political force of forty years ago, although in some parts of the Deep South, concentrating on hostility to Negroes and to racial desegregation, it has become again on the local level an effective instrument of political and economic coercion and of sheer terror.

Long, Coughlin, and the Thirties

The depression helped to end the Klan power of the 1920's, but it also produced new extremist movements of its own. One of these centered around one of the most dynamic political leaders this country has ever seen—Huey Long. Initially gathering strength only in his own state of Louisiana, before the end of his career Long was acquiring a large body of followers in neighboring states and was beginning to raise fears that his appeal might be equally effective in distant parts of the country. His assassination ended that threat, but it is worth noting that a short time earlier he had been referred to by a rather astute political observer—Franklin D. Roosevelt—as one of the two men capable of bringing the United States under totalitarian rule.

Huey Long was a curious phenomenon. He refused to conform to any standard patterns, even those of demagoguery. His highly efficient semitotalitarian rule in Louisiana was corrupt and undemocratic and was accompanied by occasional use of the methods of the police state. Such wholesale use of public power, and even violence, to quell political opposition was a new development in Louisiana, but graft and the absence of democracy were nothing new in that state. Surprisingly enough, Long refused for the most

56

part to make use of the race issue and always gained most of the Negro votes in Louisiana. His appeal was not racial, although it was primarily to that part of the Southern population which is usually highly sensitive to racial matters. Instead, his attraction was ideological, although support of him was strengthened by a great deal of sheer irrational commitment to him as a personality. Long was appealing to the large body of voters to whom economic conditions were intolerable. They always had been, but they were becoming worse, and there seemed to be no way out. Past Louisiana governments had certainly done little enough for them. Long promised them something approximating a revolution. Whether his radicalism was essentially of the left or of the right is still a matter of argument; as with most extremist movements, it was the radicalism itself which was significant, not its nominal theoretical orientation. Long certainly did upset the traditional pattern in Louisiana. Schools, highways, and bridges were built in unprecedented numbers, and taxes rose accordingly—but the taxes were mostly on those who could afford them and who would never have supported Long anyway. Even a quarter of a century after his death the name Long was political magic in his state.

Whether Huey Long could really have attained national power is not easy to say. Given the widespread and relatively effective program of relief and reform being undertaken during the 1930's by the New Deal, it seems unlikely that majorities in areas less depressed than Louisiana and adjacent states would have come to support him. Had Roosevelt or someone like him not been available—someone dedicated to the proposition that economic and social changes as drastic as those proposed by Long could be undertaken within the framework of a democracy which retained all its basic characteristics of political freedom and choice—or had the worst sort of economic privation persisted on a large scale despite the efforts at relief and reform, how far Long would have gone is anyone's guess. He certainly had most of the attributes of the successful totalitarian leader.

Equally disturbing at the time, though perhaps less serious in retrospect, were several other radical groups of the depression era. Father Charles Coughlin, who as "the Radio Priest" had gathered a large group of listeners (by no means all of them Catholic), began with wholehearted support for the New Deal, mingled with some truly extraordinary ideas on economics which caused even the most radical of New Deal planners to shudder with as much horror as the leaders of Wall Street. Whether his antagonism to capitalism stemmed from his anti-Semitism or the other way around is difficult to say, but by 1937 his antagonism to Jews and his animosity toward Roosevelt were receiving most of the emphasis. His vitriolic performances on the air were highly embarrassing to many of his fellow Catholics, and he was denounced in vigorous terms by some of them, including two cardinals and a number of prominent bishops, but his own bishop declined for several years to discipline Father Coughlin or to restrict his political activities. On specific issues he was credited with a considerable impact at the time, but his effort in 1936 to procure support for a third-party ticket, headed by Representative Lemke of North Dakota, was a conspicuous failure. Many were influenced by Coughlin, but few of these had lost all touch with political reality. Most of those who listened to him remained convinced that FDR was a pretty faithful representative of their interests. Those who did not believe this usually concluded that if there were some slim chance of defeating Roosevelt, it would be through the Republican Party, not a splinter group. Father Coughlin's determined opposition to American involvement in World War II and something very close to open support for Hitler at several junctures led by 1940 to a decline in his following and eventually to an order by the new bishop of his diocese that he terminate his political activities and confine himself to his parish duties.

The organizational outlet for Father Coughlin's anti-Semitism was the Christian Front, but it had to share the field with a variety of organizations which combined isolationism, anti-Semitism, and pro-German feeling in varying proportions. These included the Silver Shirts, the German-American Bund, and the Militant Christian Patriots, as well as the remnants of the Ku Klux Klan. The America First Committee, consisting largely of sincere isolationists and pacifists who detested Hitler and wanted no part of anti-Semitism, was nevertheless plagued by constant efforts at infiltration of its ranks by the extremists, who were occasionally successful in this endeavor. All of these organizations collapsed after Pearl Harbor, and little more has been heard of them, except for the Klan. Many of the individuals in their ranks have remained on the scene, however, and in recent years they have been active in a variety of new groups. There is no longer a Hitler for them to defend, and few of them (except for George Lincoln Rockwell's eccentric American Nazi Party) would wish to handicap their efforts by defending him if there were, but the rest of their objectives have remained more or less unmodified.

These groups undoubtedly challenged the basic unity of this country. Seeking to alter both the nature of our political system and the right of several ethnic and religious groups to exist within our society, they managed to make life quite difficult for our political leaders and for many of their fellow citizens during the 1930's. The very limited support they received was due in part to their own inept leadership, in part to the astonishing capacity of Franklin D. Roosevelt to retain the support of the American people through extremely difficult times, and in part to the development of an international situation which made them seem opposed to the vital interests and even the survival of the nation itself. Probably only Huey Long could have led them anywhere politically under any circumstances, and his death ended that possibility. Yet some of the extremist groups of our own time, a quarter of a century later, share some of the same characteristics and even some of the same personnel. We survive the strains imposed by groups like these, but we never entirely escape from them, and they leave their marks on us and on our society.

McCarthyism

Joseph McCarthy, like Huey Long, was something new on the American political scene. Like Long, he was a demagogue, but not a typical demagogue. Like Long, he appealed to hatred and divisiveness, but not in the manner used by most previous American spokesmen for hatred and bigotry. Like Long's, his attack was aimed, in the last analysis, on what has come to be called the "establishment"—those accustomed to power, influence, wealth, and prestige. As with Long, this attack was intended quite seriously and quite sincerely. Many demagogues have employed this approach for electoral purposes, but they have commonly done more talking than acting, since their strategy often involved obtaining their financial support from those whom they were nominally challenging for power, in return for making sure that the challenge never became more than nominal. But with McCarthy and Long, there was no willingness to compromise with "the enemies" or to sell out to them, for this was a fight to the death. Not the least of the parallels can be found in those deaths, which, though different in manner, were quite similar in timing. To be sure, there were also differences. Huey Long's concrete achievements were considerable, as were his political capacities, and at his death he was still on the way up, whereas McCarthy had few concrete results to show for his work and had only himself to blame for the fact that he was thoroughly discredited and rendered politically powerless before he died. Yet, of the two, it was McCarthy whose influence on the nature of American politics was the more difficult to eradicate. It is still with us.

Part of the difficulty in dealing with Joe McCarthy, both for the politician of his time and the scholar then and now, is that he cannot be related, by the wildest stretch of the imagination, to anything as coherent as an ideology. What he hated is not difficult to discover, but when one tries to find what McCarthy essentially stood *for,* he finds—nothing. There was, of course, a drive for personal political power—a drive all politicians share to a greater or lesser degree. But when one tries to learn what McCarthy would have done with more political influence and what he did with the influence he already possessed, one discovers only the negatives—the things he wanted to destroy. Here is the true revolutionary, the nihilist, the man who wants only to produce change and cares little about the character of what will follow the change.

McCarthy can be contrasted with most earlier extremist leaders in that he eschewed anti-Semitism and refused to involve himself in race politics of any variety. He himself was Catholic and his two most prominent lieutenants were Jewish; so traditional bigotry was no part of his makeup. Attacks on the Protestant clergy by his followers were motivated less by religious antagonism (most of them being delivered by a Protestant) than by conflict with the respected element in the society represented by the ministers of their churches. The more fundamentalist and less "respectable" denominations were seldom included among the victims of these attacks. Nor was Communism really what McCarthy hated—certainly not Communism as represented by the military and economic power of the Soviet Union or by the pathetically small and ineffective Communist Party of the United States. It was, incidentally, with the support of unions controlled by that party that he won his first campaign for the United States Senate. His campaign against alleged Communists was, more than anything else, a device for attacking those who had been providing political, economic, and cultural leadership for the nation, those who supported that group, and, of course, those who opposed Joe McCarthy.

Who were the members of the "establishment"—the men McCarthy hated so much? The list was long. It included the recognized political leaders of both parties, among them a number of conservatives who, for one reason or another, challenged McCarthy's right to pose as their only legitimate leader. It included, as already indicated, the Protestant clergy, except in the more fundamentalist denominations. It included the better-known academic institutions, together with their administrators, faculties, students, and alumni. (Harvard and Johns Hopkins were singled out for particular attention, but not to the exclusion of many others.) Also subject to condemnation were the leaders of a number of business and financial institutions, particularly those associated with the northeastern United States. Not even the United States Army was free of his unappreciated attentions. Eventually it was his attack on the Army, together with his denunciation of fellow senators and of his own party leadership, which produced his political downfall. His censure by the Senate could not have been accomplished without the support of some of the senators from his own Republican Party (although the few who had been openly disgusted with him all along perhaps deserve more credit than the larger number who lost patience with him only after he began attacking his *own* party and the Senate itself).

The heritage left us by McCarthyism is still very much with us. The distrust of American leadership in all fields, including our government itself and our armed services, is a legacy we have not been able to escape. So is the antagonism toward learning and education. But the most important effect produced by Joseph McCarthy, although others before him and after him have contributed to it as well, is the large minority of Americans who have lost confidence in America itself. Convinced that our system of government is defective, that it has been led by the wrong men and in the wrong direction for several decades, and that the policies of which they disapprove are not merely mistaken but are actually illegitimate and were produced by traitors or by men so stupid that they could easily be deceived and led by traitors, these Americans have come to doubt that our pattern of government is an appropriate one for the sort of world in which we live. For them, it follows logically that radical and even revolutionary changes must be made in that system to correct it. The extent to which this doctrine is accepted and the nature of some of the groups which accept it will be discussed in Chapter Four.

Joseph McCarthy himself was one of the pranks which history sometimes plays on us, but McCarthyism was a different matter. For a number of reasons, it was almost bound to appear at the time it did. Since those reasons apply to many other instances of political extremism, they should be analyzed at this point.

One was the frustration felt by members of the Republican Party at their failure to win any elections during the 1930's and 1940's. They had been accustomed to thinking of their party as the normal majority, and history from 1860 through 1928 certainly supported that view. Only two Democratic presidential candidates (Cleveland and Wilson) gained the White House during that period of almost seven decades. Each did so only under unusual circumstances, and after two terms each was replaced by another long line of Republican Presidents. Most Republicans assumed that FDR represented another such temporary departure from a normal pattern and that their party would, of course, be back in power after a term or two. When that term or two stretched into three and four, they were naturally unhappy, but the situation could still be blamed on Roosevelt personally, and the assumption was tenable that once he was out of the picture things would return to normal.

It was 1948 which really shattered them. FDR *was* gone. There was neither a depression nor a war to account for a departure from normal. Most Republicans, after that election, came to a rational conclusion and decided that the basic pattern had been altered over the course of twenty years and that it was now the Democrats who had the normal majority. The sensible course for the party out of power (and the one followed by the Democrats during most of the time they were the minority) was to hold itself in readiness to exploit mistakes made by the opposition, to run candidates likely to appeal to some members of the other party as well as one's own ranks, and to hope that—eventually—the tables would again be turned. Those who nominated Eisenhower in 1952 and 1956 were doing precisely this. For a minority of their party, this was not enough. The American people had permitted the wrong party to win elections for two straight decades. The only possible explanation was that those people had gone stark raving mad. Who had bewitched them? It could only have been "Communists"—those same educators, clergymen, and political, military, and economic leaders whom McCarthy was branding as traitors.

Contributing to the frustration felt by these Republicans (and for other reasons by some Democrats) was the perilous international situation, which produced strains to which this country had long been unaccustomed. Another factor involved some of the ethnic groups which were discussed earlier. Made sensitive on the subject of their "Americanism" by decades of political assaults by those whose ancestors got here a little earlier, some of these second-, third-, and fourth-generation Americans sought to demonstrate their superpatriotism by supporting McCarthy. Making this all the more attractive was the fact that most of those whom he was combatting were from the ranks of the social and ethnic elements from which the later immigrants and their descendants had suffered a great deal. Revenge could therefore be combined with a convincing demonstration of their final "Americanization."

It must be emphasized that only a minority within any of these groups—Republican Party, those disturbed about an international pattern oriented to nuclear war, and Irish-Americans (or German-Americans or other ethnic elements)—supported McCarthy, and he had a few followers among people who fell in none of these categories. His impact was far greater than the number of those who followed him, however. He and his associates made the conduct of successful foreign policy and even of military planning extremely difficult during the last years of the Truman Administration and all but impossible during Eisenhower's first term. He distracted the attention of the country and of its leaders from urgent and pressing problems, such as foreign policy, national defense,

64

economic development, and race relations. Americans have been regretting the failure to deal with these ever since. And his career was a significant step in the rise of the radical right, which has been such a disturbing feature of the political scene in recent years.

4. Does an American Consensus Exist Today?

$\mathcal{T}$he historical attacks on the American consensus with which we have dealt have left their scars on our political system, but that system has managed to survive them. The task of defending what is vital in that system is never one from which we can relax very long. It is always subject to new assaults, and we must mobilize to deal with new crises as soon as old ones are past. Four of those challenges are particularly significant today; each of them threatens the basic consensus which enables our society to act as a unit. Each has its antecedents in past political and social conflicts, but each is present today in a new and different form. Some of them present more serious problems than others, but each, if left to fester in the American body politic, would gravely jeopardize its future. It is therefore vital to understand the implications of these problems. Once we gain an adequate appreciation of their origins, dimensions, and possible consequences, we shall be much better prepared to deal with them. As with our past failures of unity, the most difficult steps to be taken in solving these problems are the steps of learning what the problem really is and gaining the determination to bring it to an end.

Acceptance of the Negro

Without doubt, the most dangerous internal problem this country faces today concerns the place of the Negro in American society. For one hundred years we have been committed as a nation to the proposition that Americanism is not limited along racial lines. Most of our population subscribe to that proposition, although they may quarrel, and often do, over precisely how it applies to specific cases and how it is to be implemented in general. A minority of our white population, however, has never accepted the validity of this proposition, nor have many American Negroes ever become convinced that our nation really supports it.

From the 1880's through the 1930's American sincerity in this matter could be legitimately questioned, for during that period little occurred to indicate that we proposed to make good on this commitment. Negroes themselves lacked the political power in the South to alter the situation, nor did they possess the leadership, the organizational tools, or the educational resources with which to develop such political power. In the North they were not present in sufficient numbers to possess decisive political influence in any state or in any but a few cities, although in scattered places hints already indicated that their voting strength might some day be important enough to exert some leverage on their behalf. Among Northern whites, although there were always a few to prod sensitive consciences with the reminder that millions of fellow citizens were unable to share in most of the benefits of being American, because of their color, the dominant attitude was one of grudging acceptance of racial equality in principle and of absolute refusal to worry about the problem at all in practice. In the South a large part of the white population refused to accept the notion of racial equality in any sense and, by implication, denied that Negroes were human, although that same conscience-pricking minority was present there, as in the rest of the country.

World War II produced a drastic and sudden change in race

67

relations. (In retrospect, one can see indications at an earlier time that something new was coming in American race relations, but the process was speeded up so enormously during the early 1940's that it is perhaps proper to date the present era in the position of the Negro from that time.) For one thing, the economic position of the Negro improved almost overnight. The crying need for additional personnel to man defense plants gave him access to jobs which had always previously been denied to his race. This greatly speeded the movement of Negroes from the rural South to urban centers, both Southern and Northern, although that migration had long been under way at a slower pace. Although segregation persisted in the armed forces, Negroes there were given more responsible positions than had been open to them in the past. (The real break in the armed services came with the Korean War.) They knew, and so did many whites, that they had played a significant role in winning the war. In addition, the slow educational advances achieved over many decades were beginning to produce a corps of Negro leaders equipped to deal with the political system on a new basis, especially in the North, where those educational opportunities were much greater, though still seldom equal to those available to whites. That same educational process was developing greater political sophistication also among the rest of the Negro population.

As a result of these developments Negroes after World War II were in a position to attempt to achieve goals which would have been utterly impossible for them a few years earlier. Although only a few had reached a standard of living equal to the average among whites, most of the rest had made economic gains which made them, for the first time, an economic force of enough importance to make business leaders consider them seriously. Equally important was their new political position. In those cities and states in which they were present in substantial numbers, their votes began to assume an importance which politicians ignored at considerable risk. Even in the South, despite the great obstacles often placed in their way through legal subterfuges, economic pressure, and sheer physical terror, an expansion in Negro suffrage was definitely taking place, especially in the larger cities. Wherever Negroes possess the ballot they have something with which to bargain, and this has often been the only basis on which they could undertake any effective negotiating with the political leaders of a largely white community.

All of these developments, however, would have helped American Negroes very little had there not been at the same time a major change in the attitude of large numbers of whites. The beginnings of these changes too can be spotted in earlier years, resulting in large part from the efforts of that small group which had long been seeking to awaken the American public to its responsibilities in this area. Working largely through literature, the educational system, and the churches, they were able to boast of very few concrete results before 1940, but subtle changes in American thinking were beginning to take place, nevertheless. This process was aided substantially by the nature of our most important enemy during World War II—Germany. The savage programs of brutality toward entire racial and religious groups, including the attempted (and very nearly successful) extermination of the Jewish populations of many European countries, became an obvious target for our propaganda. For many Americans it was a short step from the condemnation of Hitler's policies in this area to a realization that our own country was not entirely without fault in the same regard. Relatively few became crusaders for better treatment of American Negroes, but many became much more sympathetic toward efforts in this direction launched by others.

The report of President's Truman's Committee on Civil Rights in 1947 was a significant indication that we once more considered ourselves committed, as a nation, to making the equality of our fellow Americans of African extraction real and not merely formal. Reinforcing this decision and aiding in its implementation was a long series of judicial decisions, of which we have not yet come

69

to the end. The most significant of these was the holding of the Supreme Court in 1954 in Brown *v.* Board of Education that legally enforced racial segregation in public schools constituted a denial of the equal protection of the laws guaranteed to every person by the Fourteenth and Fifth Amendments. The passage of civil rights legislation on three occasions between 1958 and 1964 indicated that the American legislative branch of government was not at odds with our executive and judicial institutions. The bill passed in the last of these years applied at the national level the steps taken toward equalization of treatment in public accomodations and employment by a number of states and cities beginning in the middle 1940's.

The demands of the Negro himself and the means employed to try to achieve these goals underwent considerable modification, especially from about 1960 on. Objectives which had earlier been limited, at least for tactical purposes, to equality of treatment by governmental institutions themselves, were expanded to include treatment by private firms whose business dealings put them on something of a public footing. The earlier approach, which emphasized litigation, lobbying, and political maneuvering, was continued, but it came to be supplemented, first in the Deep South and later in other regions, by large-scale direct action. The drive for Negro rights, which had earlier been the responsibility of a limited group of leaders, of whom many, though by no means all, were white, had become the responsibility of nearly the entire Negro population, and campaigns which had earlier been confined to courtrooms and legislative halls began to involve boycotts, demonstrations, mass meetings, and sit-ins. A new phase had been reached.

The Negro is, in a very real sense, the crucial test of American democracy. The element which has distinguished American society from most others has been our insistence that in this country a general pattern of equality of treatment in political, economic, and social realms does exist. We have never pretended that the results of that treatment will always be equal, for personal characteristics do enter the picture and vary a great deal from individual to individual. But we have claimed (and it has been a large part of our claim to greatness) that enough equality of opportunity was present in the United States to insure advancement and success to anyone whose individual qualities did not themselves deny him the goals he set for himself. Our performance in this respect has never been perfect, of course, but we have accomplished a great deal more than many societies have even tried. For the Negro, we have never even come close to our ideal. Nothing remotely approximating equality of opportunity exists or ever has existed for the vast majority of members of this ethnic group, although there has certainly been improvement from time to time and a great deal of improvement in the last two decades. For us to give up and to admit that the achievement of which we have boasted is possible only for some groups and not for others is to deny the validity of the principle of equality itself. It is to insist, in the language of Orwell, that, "Some men are more equal than others." And it leaves us without the ethical justification which has been such an important factor in America's strength and leadership in the past.

There are other and perhaps more practical reasons why this country cannot afford to continue to deny to Negroes full membership in our society. The damage done to American foreign policy has been described many times (and perhaps overstressed). Probably more important is the extent to which this problem, until it is permanently resolved, will continue to distract our attention from a wide variety of pressing problems, including poverty, automation, economic growth, improvement of education, the financing of medical care. Already this problem has contributed in very large part to the failure of much of the South to improve the standard of living of its population at as rapid a pace as that in the rest of the United States. It is absurd to pretend that the same problem cannot hinder the rest of the country in the same way in years to come unless we manage to solve it effectively and promptly. Significantly enough, in those Southern states which have made the most serious efforts to grant as fully as possible the demands of their Negro citizens, economic growth at a level competitive with the rest of the country has been continuing. In such states as Alabama and Mississippi, where such demands have been resisted most strenuously, economic progress has virtually halted.

Most crucial of all is the impact of racial conflict upon the basic unity of the American people. It forces us to fight over the very principles of equality and freedom which should be serving as the most important basis of that unity. It causes each of us to lose something of the morale which would otherwise stem from the confidence that our nation truly practices the principles to which many others can only aspire. If it costs us the respect of observers even in those countries which are most like us and most closely tied to us, it costs us far more in *self*-respect. We cannot turn back now and try to ignore this question once more, as we largely succeeded in doing when the Negro was confined geographically, for the most part, to the South and when he lacked the political tools with which to bring himself forcefully to our attention. There is now no way in which we can try to pretend that the race problem does not really exist. If we were to try to do so, American Negroes possess the capacity to create disturbances substantial enough to make life far less pleasant for all Americans.

As with all groups, our only guarantee that such disturbances will not take place on a large scale is the continuing confidence of most Negroes that through the exercise of their own political rights within the established democratic system and with the sympathetic co-operation of a large part of the white population there will come a time relatively soon when complexion constitutes no obstacle to any goal to which any Negro may aspire on his individual merits. If the majority of politically sophisticated Negroes ever cease to possess that faith, if they ever come to believe that they have nothing to lose because there is no way in which they can advance themselves within the framework of a society in which whites are a majority, then we will have civil conflict on a frightening scale. To avert this, our best bet is to make certain that each of the groups which might be tempted to rupture the American consensus has so much at stake within the system itself that the advantages it has gained and is certain to gain in the future are far too impressive to be risked through civil disturbances. For the Negro, this has been true largely in terms of the promises made to him concerning a better tomorrow. The time has come to make good on those promises; tomorrow has been postponed long enough and more than long enough.

The danger that Negro leadership will pass into the hands of the Black Muslims and others who themselves deny the possibility of a biracial society is very real. It becomes much greater with every Negro who becomes convinced that the efforts of more moderate leaders, including those from the Urban League, the National Association for the Advancement of Colored People, and the Southern Christian Leadership Conference, cannot succeed in gaining them a real place of dignity, honor, and well-being in America. The result may be the same if those efforts appear to be successful for only a small minority of Negroes. This threat has already forced moderate Negro leaders themselves to employ techniques which are not in all cases well adapted to the task at hand. The direct action approach, which was eminently sound and thoroughly justified when used in Southern communities in which ordinary political channels were completely closed to Negroes, may be unnecessary and therefore unjustified when used in another city in which the ordinary political processes may be used by Negroes and their organizations, as well as the rest of the population. (This criticism is not aimed at rallies, unobstructive picketing, and other devices the effect of which is merely to call attention to the demands of the group in question; these are normal adjuncts to the political process. On the other hand, efforts to obstruct access or to interfere with public transportation or with the use of streets and sidewalks, even though nonviolent, are hardly in the

73

same category and are difficult to justify except in the extreme circumstances of general denial of opportunity to protest or to exert political influence in any other way.)

For the Negro who has become convinced that America has nothing to offer to him, and whose sheer frustration may cause him to react with obstruction and even violence, this analysis will seem silly. He has the weight of considerable historical experience on his side, although his position can lead to no improvement and to the loss of even those limited gains which his race has made. To the whites, mostly but not entirely Southern, to whom their presumed superiority to Negroes is the most significant factor in their entire lives and outweighs in importance all other considerations combined, talk of consensus will be equally meaningless. But there is a majority in both races—probably a large majority—which falls into neither of these categories. Some care very little one way or the other about this question. Others have feelings, even strong feelings, in one direction or the other, but those emotions are balanced against equally strong feelings on any of a variety of other issues.

To whites in this category who are unhappy about changes in their relationship with Negroes, it must be made clear that further resistance jeopardizes many other interests which are still important to them, such as economic prosperity, public education, and the general maintenance of law and public order, not merely in racial matters but in all others. To Negroes impatient for more rapid progress and anxious to apply to any and all matters in which they are frustrated the techniques which have acquired a reputation for effectiveness in the desperate situation of a hostile and intransigent Southern town, it must be made clear that the racial gains which they have made, as well as their interests of a nonracial character, are similarly risked if they antagonize large parts of the white population with an excessive emphasis on direct action while progress, albeit distressingly slow progress, is being made through more traditional techniques. So long as the majority in

74

both races chooses to follow a rational course and to limit the scope of political action on this issue to what will not jeopardize their own valuable interests in other areas, the basic consensus will survive. To the minority in both races (even though it may be a majority in a specific locale) which refuses to follow the path of moderation and which chooses to employ violence, coercion, and terror in order to support what it considers to be an absolute moral position, subject to no negotiation, regardless of the decisions of any of the institutions of our government, it must be made clear that essential national unity will be maintained, by force if it cannot be done in any other way, even among those who refuse to be part of that consensus.

Religious Friction

There have been, in recent years, some extremely hopeful signs in connection with political relationships among holders of differing religious views. The bitter anti-Catholicism of the nativist era is now a thing of the past, so far as a very large majority of the American public is concerned. As late as 1928 this attitude was still prevalent enough to insure the denial of the Presidency to a Catholic candidate (although several other factors shared in producing the widespread hostility to Al Smith, and the Democrats would have been unlikely to win in that year anyway). By 1960 the situation was substantially different. The strenuous efforts which were made to persuade American Protestants that John F. Kennedy's election would result in the establishment of a direct phone line from the Vatican to the White House over which all instructions relevant to American policies would be transmitted and that the College of Cardinals would immediately replace the Cabinet as the major body of official advisers to the President failed to deny him the nation's highest office. (The best evidence suggests that it did cost him some three or three and a half million normally Democratic Protestant votes, for which the one or one and a half million normally Republican Catholic votes which he received were inadequate compensation. Still, it did not prevent him from winning, and the experience of the Kennedy Presidency will almost surely prevent this form of bigotry from playing an equally important role in any future national election.)

Organized anti-Semitism has undergone a similar decline, although it has certainly not disappeared from the American scene and is supplemented by occasional acts of private hostility toward Jews. The vicious literature and speeches so common in this field in an earlier time are a little more difficult to find today, although it is an unmitigated tragedy that such despicable propaganda is still around at all. There is an increasing tendency for those who have and profess anti-Semitic attitudes to be at least partially apologetic for this fact, and what in fact is anti-Semitism more often masquerades as something else. This phenomenon is no more attractive under any other label, but an attitude for which one is apologetic and which one attempts to conceal, both from himself and from others, surely has less political force than a view which is professed proudly and openly.

As suggested in an earlier chapter, part of the explanation for the decline of religious controversy in American politics is to be found in terms of a decline in the extent to which most Americans are willing to apply views based on religion to matters outside their churches. Relatively few Americans take religious doctrine with the seriousness found more often in an earlier generation. This watering down of theology at the popular level is certainly not an unmixed blessing and is properly a matter of great concern to serious religious leaders, but it does simplify the task of keeping the members of competing religious groups away from each other's throats. As religion has become vague and farther removed from most individual concerns, it has become less important to fight about it. Having been reduced to the lowest common denominator applicable to all of the large and influential denominations, the overwhelmingly "Christian" character of America has come to mean very little in specific terms. In most areas of public policy it conveys few clues as to the nature of that policy. (An exception is to be found in connection with the race issue—one of the few questions on which there has been in the last few years something close to unity of opinion among the leading denominations at the national level. Even here the impact of organized religion has been quite limited, and most churches were very slow in entering the struggle at all, although many individual clergymen and laymen, influenced by their religious convictions, did play courageous and significant roles from the beginning.)

A prominent Baptist clergyman and educator may have put the matter rather effectively when testifying before a legislative committee in opposition to a policy desired on doctrinal grounds by many members of his denomination. Asked by a legislator whether he did not believe the policy was appropriate because America was a Christian nation, he replied, "No, I do not. I have labored all my life to make this country Christian, but I am under no illusion that I have succeeded." On those matters on which a formal gesture toward religious ends can be achieved without antagonizing any major Christian denomination (and usually without alienating any significant non-Christian but theistic group), we are usually happy to do so. We are delighted to include references to the Deity in our pledge of allegiance and on our coins, and we utter public prayers on many occasions when they seem to some devout Christians to be unseemly and inappropriate. But when we come to questions which have genuine religious content and which therefore involve potentially deep and serious conflicts among large religious bodies, we do not dare to deal with them in any but the most gingerly fashion, if at all. By making it possible to avoid political decisions involving such potentially serious conflicts, our policy of separation of church and state makes an extremely significant contribution to American political stability. Unity would be far more difficult to preserve if our government were constantly making decisions in areas where our great variety of churches were in conflict and on issues which each of them regarded as fundamental to its theology and vital to its survival.

Although the Supreme Court decisions regarding the use of prayers in the public schools have been subjected to widespread attack by a few religious leaders and by a great many other people who regard themselves, without any particular authority for doing so, as spokesmen for their own churches, these judicial decisions are a significant element in the struggle to keep matters of religious doctrine out of the political arena. To the individual to whom prayer is seriously meaningful, it is a matter closely related to deeply held beliefs and feelings. If he takes his religion seriously, many of these are by no means the same beliefs and feelings characteristic of other religious groups, whom he may respect but with whom he must continue to disagree on quite profound questions. To such an individual, the so-called nonsectarian prayer is really no prayer at all, for it is devoid of the religious elements which to him are important. The defense of prayers and of Bible reading on the ground that they really do not have much to do with religion is little short of blasphemy.

For the sincere member of any religious group, the differences which divide his church from others are of genuine importance. For such an individual, prayers will either reflect those differences from time to time or they will have no significance as prayers. If the latter is the case, there can be no real argument for making them part of the school program. If, on the other hand, a prayer is to have some serious religious content and therefore to reflect the doctrines of one church as opposed to others, there would seem to be no way of avoiding the problem of which denomination is to prevail. In any community in which one church is dominant, the practical answer is likely to be that it will control the character of religious observances in the schools, the wishes and beliefs of members of other sects to the contrary notwithstanding. In those communities in which different denominations are more evenly balanced, constant conflict is more likely to be the result. If they take turns, the result for young students will surely be one of confusion, possibly leading in turn to cynicism. This can be avoided only by diluting the religious content of the prayers and other observances to the point at which they offend no members of other churches and are therefore meaningless.

The sensible line would seem to be that suggested by the Supreme Court, leaving the individual free to determine, in concert with his church, the time and manner of his prayers and other religious observances, and leaving governmental institutions free of the responsibility for making decisions among competing religious sects as to which is the correct version of the scriptures and what prayers are to be said rather than others. If religion were to become again an important force in American life, the making of such decisions through political means would be bound to produce the same sort of civil dispute over theological principles which created turmoil in Europe during the sixteenth and seventeenth centuries.

The Radical Right

An overtly political challenge to the basis of the American consensus comes from what has come to be called the Radical Right. Sometimes confused with ordinary political conservatives, these groups, of which the most prominent has been the John Birch Society, may be distinguished by their denial of the validity of the basic political framework within which we have been operating. The traditional conservative accepts that framework and acknowledges the legitimacy of decisions made by the regularly selected leaders of the political system, even though he personally has opposed their elections or appointments and even though he disapproves of the particular decisions being made. The radical, however, even though he is from the right rather than from the left, wishes to produce a revolutionary change in the nature of the constitutional system. He believes that American society

79

has fallen to such a low point that corrective action cannot be taken through existing governmental institutions, so long as they are subject to democratic control. Possessing the courage of his convictions, he believes that a political structure which permits the "wrong" decisions to be made is intolerable and ought to be replaced with one which responds to the "correct" moral and political forces and which therefore allows only the "right" decisions to be made. The fact that other parts of the American population do not share their views as to the ethical validity of certain decisions seems to them to be utterly beside the point.

The John Birch Society itself, at least at the level of its national leadership, has made strenuous efforts to avoid racism and religious bigotry. Many of the other organizations on the far right have had no such inhibitions and have been happy to share in the anti-Semitism and the violent hostility toward Negroes of the Ku Klux Klan, and some of them, especially in the South, have had little else to offer. True, they have joined the Birchers in designating "Communism" as the enemy, but they have made it abundantly clear that a Communist, in their definition, is a person who is willing to permit some changes in the role of the Negro in American society and particularly in their communities.

For any part of the Radical Right, however, some aspect of contemporary American government is intolerable. If it is not the changing pattern of race relations which offends, it is the role of organized labor, or the decline of religious fundamentalism, or the evils of progressive education, or governmental regulation of economic activities. Other political crimes of which they complain include social welfare programs and the unwillingness of recent administrations to run even graver risks of war in order to secure foreign-policy goals which are construed, at the very least, as including the immediate removal of "Communist" influence from all areas to which it has spread since the beginning of World War II. (Many refuse to draw the line at that point and will tolerate no foreign-policy gestures which seem likely to stop short of the restoration of a "friendly" regime in the Soviet Union itself, although an appropriate candidate for Tsar seems to have eluded them as yet.)

To each of the members of the extreme right, one or more of these situations seems to justify the abandonment or drastic restriction of democratic government and of many of the constitutional arrangements developed over the course of almost two centuries in this country. They are particularly distressed over the fact that not only can such "wicked" policies be promulgated in our country, but they can actually be defended before the public, not only by the "evil" or "Communist" political leaders themselves but through educational institutions, churches, and the media of communications. Consequently, all of those are also subject to wholesale denunciation, and the provisions of the Bill of Rights which protect these institutions and their members, as well as the rest of the public, are regarded as essentially subversive.

By examining the actual institutions and individuals attacked by these groups, we gain impressive evidence of the basically revolutionary character of these extremists. Like Joseph McCarthy and his associates a decade earlier (and the overlap in personnel between the more vehement of McCarthy's followers and some of these groups is very great), these organizations maintain, largely to themselves, the fiction that they are seeking to preserve and to promote what they call "Americanism." But most of what can honestly be termed American is on their list of subversive influences. Very few of our national leaders—political, religious, economic, educational, or cultural—have escaped their vitriolic denunciations. Such vital American traditions as the supremacy of civil over military authority, the rule of law, the importance of public education, the separation of church and state, and the values of intellectual liberty and the freedom of speech and of the press have been repudiated by these organizations. Even their claim to be defending capitalism and "free enterprise" must be doubted by anyone who, like this author, has heard a John Birch leader denounce in violent language the influence on the Republican Party of "those damned Wall Street Communists!"

Clearly enough, the sort of America which these people would like to produce is one quite unlike the America we have today. Nor are they classical reactionaries, anxious to restore, as faithfully as they can, a society which existed at an earlier time but which has now vanished. The ideal of the Radical Right does indeed contain some elements which can be found in an earlier America, but the pattern as a whole is a revolutionary one for which no earlier precedent is to be found in our history. The changes which they seek involve little or nothing in the way of continuity with that history. Instead, like McCarthy, they find themselves alienated from American society and culture in certain fundamental ways, and they identify the institutions and leaders of that society as their enemies.

Modern America has emphasized such values as religious tolerance, racial compatibility, the maximum of individual freedom in intellectual and cultural matters, the importance of education and intellectual effort, the settlement of internal conflict through peaceful political processes, and the supremacy of law, determined and applied under the standards we know as due process. Modern America is an urban society, with an urban culture. Modern America stresses the necessity of achieving for every American the maximum possible standard of living. Modern America insists that that standard of living, although by no means equal for all our citizens, can undergo steady improvement for all of them for an indefinite time to come. The members of the Radical Right, unable to adjust to this society, must seek instead to bring it to an end.

Although their members have disagreements among themselves on specific points, the groups of the extreme right share in general a commitment to most or all of the following principles. They would substitute for religious toleration an insistence on uniform acceptance not only of Christianity but of their particular highly dogmatic version of Christianity. They would replace the ideal of freedom for Americans of all races with a claim for complete and permanent white superiority and supremacy. They demand a maximum of cultural conformity, and the culture which they find to their liking is one based on the values of the small towns in which relatively few Americans live and in which only a minority of present-day Americans have ever lived. They deny the value of education and intellectual activities, except for professional and technical training, the traditional elementary courses, and indoctrination in their own political and religious philosophies, usually presented under the guise of patriotism or "Americanism." For the rule of law and the acceptance of the lawful decisions of legislative and administrative bodies and the courts, subject to their possible change later through equally lawful procedures, they would substitute disrespect for judges and those political leaders of whom they disapprove and the freedom to ignore those laws and judicial decisions with which they are not in agreement. Rather than an improvement in the economic position of all Americans, they urge the need to maintain drastic differences in income levels among Americans, and to this end they support policies which would have the effect of insuring a permanently low standard of living for many of our citizens.

The conflict between these views and those of most Americans is quite obvious. Despite the insistence of the rightists that they stand for individualism and liberty, it is a conflict between authoritarianism on their side and an open, relatively free, and largely democratic society on the other. Although some people who identify themselves with right-wing groups are careful to stop short of the totalitarian implications of the extreme rightist position (and most do so in the particular case of economic activity), there is a basic antagonism between their principles and the democratic side of the American tradition. This antagonism is emphasized by those leaders of the far right who have openly insisted that democracy and "Americanism" are incompatible and who have attempted unsuccessfully to demonstrate that democracy is contrary to the American historical pattern and is a subversive influence introduced in this country only in relatively recent years.

Although some observers have expressed fears that a takeover by the Radical Right in the United States is a real danger—either through the democratic electoral process itself or through non-constitutional means, possibly with the assistance of some elements in the armed services—those fears appear at the present time to be somewhat exaggerated. For one thing, inept leadership in most of the right-wing groups has led to simultaneous attacks on all the aspects of American society which they scorn. This has produced much more widespread, better-organized, and more effective opposition to them than they need otherwise have encountered at this time. They might have been better advised to tackle one set of enemies at a time, rather than allying many groups against them, while making it clear to all political elements from traditional conservatives to liberals that the rightists constitute a force hostile to them and to the political framework within which they have been operating. Still another defect in the planning of the Radical Right has been their inability to resolve some significant conflicts among their own groups. This problem could conceivably be solved at any time, since it has developed more out of personality conflicts among leaders than out of any fundamental differences in ideology.

Most important, the climate of opinion in the United States at present is not conducive to a rapid increase in the power of the extreme right. The sort of situation which Hitler was able to exploit in Germany in the early 1930's is simply not in existence in the United States in the middle 1960's. Some of the right-wing spokesmen obviously believe that violent white reaction to the political and economic gains being made by Negroes will create such turmoil and unrest that existing political institutions will collapse and they will be able to step in and pick up the pieces, but considerable evidence suggests that general lawlessness and disorder will not develop out of this problem, even in the Deep South. A widespread economic collapse, such as that of the 1930's, would greatly alter the situation, but it is fairly clear that such is not impending, nor are we likely to place in office at the national level an administration which would permit it. The only other eventuality which would lead to the sort of chaos which the extreme right could easily exploit would be the aftermath of a nuclear war. One of the right-wing organizations, the Minutemen, appears to base most of its planning on the assumption that such an event is coming in the near future. Most of the rest of us, while admitting the all too tragic possibility of such an occurrence, are not willing to grant that it is inevitable and are certainly not willing to confine our political thinking to the problem of how to seize power after such a war.

On the whole, therefore, the Radical Right, although presenting a basic challenge to the American consensus, cannot, under present circumstances, make that challenge a successful one. The need to deal effectively with this force in the political arena is nevertheless urgent, because we cannot be absolutely certain that the political environment will not change so as to favor extremist movements and because it is always necessary to make clear, on a continuing basis, that the American commitment to liberty, democracy, political and legal equality, and stable constitutional government is firm and lasting.

Foreign Policy and American Consensus

A consensus on an appropriate American foreign policy for the present time does, in broad outline, exist, although that policy must necessarily undergo constant revision and modification in detail as circumstances change. The four administrations since the end of World War II—those of Truman, Eisenhower, Kennedy, and Johnson—have all followed the same general line in this area. The most obvious indication of the extent to which this is true is the fact that both Eisenhower and Kennedy, though elected in large part on the basis of campaign commitments in the field of foreign affairs, undertook no drastic alterations in the international policies developed by their predecessors. In general, American foreign policy since a time shortly after the end of World War II has been built around the need to resist the expansion of Soviet (and since 1950 Chinese) power by providing assurances of the availability of American military forces to resist aggression where such resistance is feasible, by promoting stability in areas not immediately subject to Soviet or Chinese intervention but in which they might eventually see fit to expand their influence, and by seeking to loosen the control of the two hostile powers over nations already within their spheres of influence.

We have sought to do all this while avoiding acts which we suspect would be so intolerable to the leaders of the Soviet Union that they would accept World War III rather than permit us to carry out our policies. At the same time, we have made it clear to the other side that there are limits to what we ourselves will permit without resorting to general war, and we have sought to insure that our own power, supplemented by that of our allies, remained at all times adequate to enable us to fight such a war if it should be precipitated. At the same time, we have not tried to provoke such a war over interests which were not in fact vital to us. Since the Russians have at most times based their policies on similar considerations, the period since 1945 has seen neither an all-out war nor a surrender by either side of positions deemed vital to national survival.

On both sides of the struggle which we have called the Cold War these policies have been widely criticized. Openly in China and behind the scenes in the Soviet Union, Russian leadership under Khrushchev and his successors has been condemned for cowardice, indecision, and lack of determination to win the conflict. This argument has taken two forms. First, it is alleged, the West would always back down and surrender if convinced that thermonuclear war were the only alternative. Second, it is argued, the United States and its European allies are not nearly as powerful as they would appear on the surface and would therefore be defeated decisively in such a war if they dared to fight it.

Ironically, precisely the same criticisms are directed at American foreign policy and for the corresponding contradictory reasons. It is argued that if we were only willing to go ahead and indicate that we fully intend to commence a full-scale thermonuclear war if the Russians and Chinese do not immediately surrender to us on every point which has the slightest significance to us in international politics, there would be no need to fight such a war, for the Russians and Chinese would never dare to do so. This presumes that there are no matters which to their leaders are important enough to be worth fighting about—a highly dubious proposition. Alternatively, it is insisted that we could easily win such a war without paying an excessive price for such a victory, even though most of our allies might well refuse to join us in a conflict in which we were in large part the aggressors. This presumes that neither Russia nor China possesses any truly significant military power—an equally dubious proposition. These indictments of American foreign policy over the last two decades come largely from the Radical Right, but they are also voiced from time to time by people who do not share the extremist position on other matters. For that reason, this problem deserves separate treatment in this analysis.

Most Americans do not share these views. Most Americans remain committed to the proposition that there are vital American interests which must be protected, even at considerable risk of war. There are very few who argue that we ought to be willing under any circumstances to yield our national independence or our ability to protect ourselves militarily from any likely threat. Even areas outside our boundaries, such as Western Europe, without which we would in the long run find it extremely difficult or even impossible to defend ourselves, have been placed in the category of areas on which a military attack will be regarded as an act of war against the United States. At the same time, most Americans agree that, if at all possible, the protection of our vital interests ought to be accomplished without war and without unnecessary risk of war. To a lesser degree, they also accept the idea that even if war is necessary, it ought, if possible, to be kept limited in scope and intensity.

Foreign policy is certainly not free from the necessity of intelligent criticism. Mistakes are made from time to time, in this area as in others, and they ought to be corrected. Policies which are appropriate in one period become obsolete and need to be overhauled or replaced in another. The extremist criticism of which we have been speaking is another matter, however, for it suggests that the policies of all recent administrations have been not only mistaken but intended to betray us, that they have been produced by traitors and the dupes of traitors, and that any problems which have not been completely solved in international relations can be accounted for only by the faults of our own leaders. This belief is based on a profound misconception of the realities of international relations. From the correct idea that the United States is the most powerful nation in the world, these critics have jumped to the erroneous notion that our power is infinite. They also assume that the existence of continuing conflict is evidence of the failure of our policies, whereas a more realistic view is that conflict is inevitable so long as there are separate nations. All that foreign policy can accomplish is to limit the scope and number of such conflicts and to advance and protect our interests as far as possible despite the existence of such conflicts. This approach limits the gains which are possible for us and recognizes that we will never achieve an ideal situation in our relations with other nations, but it also limits the most appalling of our risks and maximizes the possibility of protecting at least the most vital of our interests.

Just as important as the particular approach to foreign policy which the United States has been using for two decades and which is supported by this analysis is the need to keep the determination and administration of all our policies within a constitutional framework accepted by the American people. To cast doubt upon the validity of the decisions made by the highest officers of our government and to suggest that our chief national leaders, elected by the American people or appointed by those who are so elected, have no authority to commit the United States to any policies of which these critics disapprove is to make the task of those leaders so difficult that it sometimes seems doubtful to foreign observers that our leaders are representing the United States at all. Yet it is absolutely vital that we have personnel who can speak for America and who can commit it to given courses of action in international affairs. If the extremists make this impossible, they will have caused far more harm to their country than any number of mistakes in specific policies would be likely to produce.

The Consensus Survives

The challenges to American unity which have been discussed in this chapter are not, of course, the only ones which could be found, but they are the most serious threats to the American consensus which are to be found at the present time. Although our society seems capable at the moment of dealing effectively with all of these threats, each of them—racism, religious clashes, the Radical Right, and the battle over foreign policy—could, under different circumstances, destroy the American pattern as we have known it.

A question will no doubt be raised as to why the extremists of the left are not included among the threats to the basis of American government and society. Is it because there are no such extremists? Obviously enough, there are. Is it because their attacks involve no fundamental conflict with the American consensus? On the contrary, the Communists and others who uphold the doctrine of violent revolution or who deny the basic legitimacy of our system of government and the policies which it produces present, in theory, just as much of a challenge to American democracy as the John Birchers and other extremists of the right. Thirty years ago that challenge was not merely theoretical but actual, for the depression produced rapid growth in political extremes of all kinds. Long, Coughlin, and others of the right did not have the field to themselves, although they proved far more effective at exploiting the situation than the ineptly led Communist Party of the United States. Since then, that party has continued to go downhill, discredited by the absurd gyrations of the party line under Stalin, by the general prosperity of a large majority of Americans since 1940, and by the consistent support it has given the Soviet Union in its conflict with this country since 1945.

Not by the wildest stretch of the imagination is that party today in a position to create any serious political problems within this country. Like other political situations, this one might change, but it is difficult to conceive of anything short of a successful Soviet invasion and occupation of the United States which would lead to a significant political role for the American Communist Party. (To judge from the extent to which Soviet Communists appear to regard the American variety as little children playing at the serious business of politics, even that might not follow.) It is not their philosophy but their political weakness and incompetence which prevents our domestic Communists from constituting a real threat to American unity.

We must beware of classing as extremists all those whose political views are to the left or right of center on the American political spectrum. Extremism, for our purposes, is determined not by the particular policies which one supports but by refusal to work within the limits of the constitutional system and the democratic political process and the refusal to accept as binding the policy decisions of which one disapproves, even though they are made through the legitimate procedures of the system. The thoroughgoing Marxist who urges the immediate nationalization of all industry but who is willing to admit that so far he has not succeeded in persuading Congress, the President, or the American public to do this and that until he does it is perfectly legitimate for such industry to remain within private or corporate hands remains within the pattern of consensus. Dissent and disagreement are vital elements in our system, provided the dissenter is willing to wait until he gains general support before he insists on placing his principles in operation (even though he recognizes the possibility that he will be waiting forever).

The same mistake, of equating a strong policy position with an intolerable challenge to the basic nature of the political system, is sometimes made with regard to the right. There are many staunch conservatives, disappointed or even disgusted with much that has happened in this country over the last thirty (or one hundred and thirty) years, who nevertheless grant that the policies which distress them were adopted through proper procedures, do not violate the basic principles of the American constitutional system, and must therefore be complied with in ungrudging though perhaps unenthusiastic fashion until and unless they can be modified through the same democratic procedures. To call such a person an extremist is absurd. He, like the liberal or the democratic socialist, accepts the principle of political obligation and respects the limits placed on political action by the necessity of maintaining an essential measure of national unity and of effective government.

It was astonishing to many foreign observers that the assassination of President John F. Kennedy did not produce a violent rupture of the American consensus. Under other circumstances, of course, it might have done so, for he was not merely a popular President but also a political figure who attracted deeper loyalties and emotional ties than any of our leaders since Franklin D. Roosevelt—deeper than any but a very few of our statesmen have managed to create. As with any political figure to whom loyalties this profound have developed, there were also those who hated him with a bitter and consuming intensity. Only Jefferson, Jackson, Lincoln, Wilson, and FDR matched Kennedy in the extent of this extraordinary and vitriolic hostility.

Unlike Lincoln, however, Kennedy was not killed because of

this hostility. (Had he been, the repercussions would almost certainly have been more violent and more extensive.) Instead, he died in a manner which made his death appear irrational and meaningless. The American public, though shocked and stunned, as was much of the rest of the world, treated the murder as an event which would not basically change the political direction of our society. Steps taken by President Johnson immediately after assuming his new office reinforced this view. Although no two Presidents are precisely alike, and their administrations cannot produce identical results, it became abundantly clear that President Johnson proposed to push ahead along lines quite similar to those indicated earlier by Kennedy. Those who had despised Kennedy (except for a few who did so solely because of his religion) found no reason to be less antagonistic toward Johnson. Those who approved of Kennedy's programs found that most of them remained in effect, many were expanded, and new policies of the same general sort were inaugurated.

So far, our society has survived, and it has maintained an acceptable degree of unity for the last century and, with the one exception of the Civil War, for almost two centuries. But this consensus has been subjected to many tests. Some of its most serious challenges face it at the present time. Our history offers no assurances that we will meet those challenges successfully. Only the awareness by Americans of the nature of these conflicts and of their possible consequences can provide such an assurance. We will, of course, discover additional problems in future years, and those too will threaten the disruption of our society. Never will we be able to relax, ignore our problems, and assume that nothing can harm us. That world of careless irresponsibility exists only in childhood. Adults who try to find it, either as individuals or as nations, encounter disaster. Conflicts and problems will beset us always, and they will never be overcome or contained except through the constant application of such capacities as we possess, both as citizens and as a society, with all the resources and energies at our command. At such a prospect, some will despair, because some can never bring themselves to act until they are assured that all will be perfect and ideal once the action is completed. For the rest of us, persuaded that the American society we know offers much that is worthwhile, it is necessary to commit all that we can to the preservation of the many things that are good about it and the correction and improvement of the aspects of this society which are defective. We are under no illusion that we will achieve heaven on earth, but we do know that things could be a great deal worse— and that unless we exert ourselves they will be.

Consequences of Consensus

Much that makes our society a relatively pleasant and attractive one in which to live stems from the consensus described in this volume. Democracy itself presumes such an underlying agreement within a country. As indicated earlier, it cannot exist on a stable basis without at least general agreement on democracy as the appropriate pattern of government. Beyond that, however, is the fact that democracy depends for its ultimate justification on consent from the population, not the mere application of superior force. That consent will not be and need not be unanimous, but it must be so general that disruptive challenges to the authority of the government, including any large-scale political violence, will be prevented or controlled through absence of popular support and, indeed, overwhelming public action to maintain or restore the authority of the government and our political stability. This implies general public acceptance of the legitimacy (though not necessarily the wisdom) of the actions of the institutions of government. Those who disagree with official policies, determined through the established constitutional procedures, are free to criticize and to work for their change but accept the necessity for complying with them until and unless they are changed. Only if this is true can a democratic system provide stable and effective government.

It is less obvious but equally true that, unless such general consent is present, *no* system of government will be stable and effective, even in accomplishing the purposes of its rulers. The sole exception is a thoroughly totalitarian, highly efficient police state, and even it must have approval from at least a sizable part of the public. All societies depend, for the effective accomplishment of any goals, on widespread agreement as to those goals and on acceptance, at least for the time being, of the means chosen by their leaders to reach those goals. Otherwise, the energies and resources present in those nations are dissipated in internal conflicts. The major usefulness of social organization, including government, comes from its capacity to enable men to combine their resources and efforts in order to achieve far more than they could individually. If such combination is not truly present, we are back with the disadvantages of anarchy and chaos.

The need for consensus in dealing with problems of foreign policy and national security is evident, but it should be noted that the consensus must be present not merely on those issues themselves but others as well. Our power in international politics is dependent in no small part on our ability to act together as a nation, and any issue which tears us apart weakens us in dealing with other countries, for it casts doubt on that national unity. This does not mean, of course, that we are in unanimous agreement on how to accomplish our foreign policy goals, but it does mean that in this field, as in domestic matters, we must insure that all foreign leaders are aware that we propose to deal with them as a national unit and that our leaders, especially the President, possess the authority to speak for us and to commit us as a nation. Unless this is true, our great power can never be effectively applied to problems of national security.

An America which remains conscious of its nationhood and of the political obligations which are essential to any nation has every reason to remain confident of its future. That future will not be secured merely by the singing of patriotic songs, the chanting of

94

slogans, and the uttering of prayers for the future greatness of our nation and the destruction of others, although these have symbolic values of importance. It will not be secured through the suppression of dissent and disagreement or through the denial of membership in our society to large groups which live here. It will not be secured through attempting to shift our fundamental loyalties from the national level to the separate states or our individual communities. It will be secured through a common acceptance of the fact of our Americanism. It will be secured through a common acceptance of the rest of our population as equally American. It will be secured through a common determination to preserve the fundamentally democratic character of our governmental system. It will be secured through a general acceptance of dissent and disagreement among others as a legitimate part of the system. It will be secured through continuing recognition of the validity of many policies with which we personally disagree and of the need to comply willingly with those policies so long as they possess legal sanction and so long as the democratic process remains available to alter them if it should seem advisable to the rest of the population to do so. Our future will not be secured by the extremists who panic and urge disruption and violence when they think of the present state of our society and the direction in which they think it is moving. It will be secured by those who accept that society as essentially good and who expect to continue to take steps, within the framework of basic patterns long established, to make it better.

The Challenge to Americans

This book suggests that challenges to American unity and democracy are by no means new. Our history is one of repeated threats of internal dissension and disruption, some of the more serious of which have been described in these pages. Problems of long standing are still with us, some of them originating before the establishment of the United States itself. Others continue to arise in our own era, and these may be equally dangerous. All of them menace the consensus on the basis of which our society manages to survive and prosper. Nor will these threats vanish in any foreseeable future. No society has ever found itself permanently free of the danger of disunity. If one such threat is eliminated or contained, others are already in view. As long as our country survives, it will have problems of this character. The duration of that survival will depend in substantial part on the effectiveness with which its leaders deal with problems of unity and the amount of understanding support along these lines which political leaders receive from other elements in the population, particularly the educated and politically active population. If we ignore these problems, they will surely overwhelm us. We cannot take national unity and political stability for granted. They will have a chance to endure only so long as we are acquainted with their foundations and appreciate the nature of the threats to the consensus which are always with us.

There is no need to despair. Despite the size, diversity, and complexity of American society, fundamental strife over the nature of our political system and the other basic issues described here *can* be kept within tolerable limits. But this will not happen automatically. It will happen only if we, the American people, acting with understanding and determination, cause it to happen. The depth of our own commitment to our nation and to democracy will decisively influence the capacity of both to survive.

BIBLIOGRAPHY

The serious reader is aware by this time that this book has touched only the top layer of an extremely broad and complex topic. It is hoped that he will wish to explore the subject much more thoroughly and from different perspectives. This list includes a variety of volumes which may prove useful in his attempt to do so. These books explore certain aspects of the subject in much greater detail. The author relied on many of them in part for his coverage of the same topics. Others present contrary views of the same matters. In either case, the reader is encouraged to carry his study of this field as far as he can. There is no pretense that this book is the last word on this vital subject. It will have served its purpose if it is, for some readers, the first.

POLITICAL OBLIGATION

Buchanan, James M. and Gordon Tullock. *The Calculus of Consent.* Ann Arbor: University of Michigan Press, 1962.

Butz, Otto. *Of Man and Politics.* New York: Holt, Rinehart & Winston, 1962.

Cook, Thomas I. *History of Political Philosophy from Plato to Burke.* New York: Prentice-Hall, 1936.

deGrazia, Sebastian. *The Political Community.* Chicago: University of Chicago Press, 1948.

Gough, J. W. *John Locke's Political Philosophy.* New York: Oxford University Press, 1950.

Hallowell, John H. *Main Currents in Modern Political Thought.* New York: Henry Holt & Co., 1950.

Kendall, Wilmoore. *John Locke and the Doctrine of Majority Rule.* Urbana: University of Illinois Press, 1941.

Laski, Harold J. *Authority in the Modern State.* New Haven: Yale University Press, 1919.

MacIver, Robert. *The Web of Government.* New York: Macmillan Co., 1947.

Sabine, George H. *A History of Political Theory.* New York: Henry Holt and Co., 1937.

Tussman, Joseph. *Obligation and the Body Politic.* New York: Oxford University Press, 1960.

Weldon, T. D. *States and Morals.* London: Whittlesey House, 1947.

POLITICAL OBLIGATION AND AMERICAN DEMOCRACY

Cantril, Hadley. *Faith, Hope, and Heresy.* Princeton: Institute for International Social Research, 1957.

Cohen, Carl (ed.). *Communism, Fascism, and Democracy.* New York: Random House, 1962.

Dahl, Robert A. *A Preface to Democratic Theory.* Chicago: University of Chicago Press, 1956.

deGrazia, Alfred. *Public and Republic.* New York: Alfred A. Knopf, 1951.

deTocqueville, Alexis. *Democracy in America.* New York: Alfred A. Knopf, 1945.

Fein, Leonard J. (ed.). *American Democracy: Essays on Image and Realities.* New York: Holt, Rinehart & Winston, 1964.

Friedrich, Carl J. *The New Image of the Common Man.* Boston: Beacon Press, 1950.

Hofstadter, Richard. *The American Political Tradition.* New York: Alfred A. Knopf, 1951.

Holcombe, Arthur. *Our More Perfect Union.* Cambridge: Harvard University Press, 1950.

Key, V. O., Jr., *Public Opinion and American Democracy.* New York: Alfred A. Knopf, 1961.

Lindsay, A. D. *The Modern Democratic State.* London: Oxford University Press, 1943.

Lippmann, Walter. *Essays in the Public Philosophy.* Boston: Little, Brown & Co., 1955.

Lipson, Leslie. *The Democratic Civilization.* New York: Oxford University Press, 1964.

Riemer, Neal. *The Revival of Democratic Theory.* New York: Appleton-Century-Crofts, 1962.

Schattschneider, E. E. *The Semi-Sovereign People.* New York: Holt, Rinehart & Winston, 1960.

Spitz, David. *Patterns of Anti-Democratic Thought*. New York: Macmillan Co., 1949.

Thorson, Thomas L. *The Logic of Democracy*. New York: Holt, Rinehart & Winston, 1962.

CHARACTER OF THE SYSTEM

Agar, Herbert. *The Price of Union*. Boston: Houghton, Mifflin Co., 1950.

Anderson, William. *The Nation and the States*. Minneapolis: University of Minnesota Press, 1955.

Beveridge, Albert J. *The Life of John Marshall*. 4 vols. Boston: Houghton, Mifflin Co., 1916–1919.

Boorstin, Daniel. *The Genius of American Politics*. Chicago: University of Chicago Press, 1953.

Burns, James M. *The Deadlock of Democracy*. Englewood Cliffs, New Jersey: Prentice-Hall, 1963.

Carr, E. H. *Nationalism and After*. New York: Macmillan Co., 1945.

Einstein, Lewis. *Divided Loyalties*. London: Cobden-Sanderson, 1933.

Hartz, Louis. *The Liberal Tradition in America*. New York: Harcourt, Brace & Co., 1955.

Huntington, Samuel P. *The Soldier and the State*. Cambridge: Harvard University Press, 1958.

Kohn, Hans. *American Nationalism*. New York: Macmillan Co., 1958.

McIlwaine, Charles H. *The American Revolution: A Constitutional Interpretation*. New York: Macmillan Co., 1923.

Rossiter, Clinton. *Conservatism in America*. New York: Alfred A. Knopf, 1955.

Rossiter, Clinton. *Seedtime of the Republic*. New York: Harcourt, Brace & Co., 1953.

Swisher, Carl B. *The Growth of Constitutional Power in the United States*. Chicago: University of Chicago Press, 1946.

Van Tyne, Claude H. *The Loyalists in the American Revolution*. New York: P. Smith, 1929.

Wright, Benjamin F. *Consensus and Continuity, 1776–1787*. Boston: Boston University Press, 1958.

Wright, Benjamin F. (ed.). *The Federalist*. Cambridge: Belknap Press of Harvard University Press, 1961.

MEMBERSHIP IN THE SOCIETY

Grodzins, Morton. *Americans Betrayed.* Chicago: University of Chicago Press, 1949.

Grodzins, Morton. *The Loyal and the Disloyal.* Chicago: University of Chicago Press, 1956.

Hyman, Herbert. *Political Socialization.* Glencoe, Illinois: Free Press, 1959.

Kornhauser, Arthur William. *The Politics of Mass Society.* Glencoe, Illinois: Free Press, 1959.

Levin, Murray B. *The Alienated Voter.* New York: Holt, Rinehart & Winston, 1960.

THE CIVIL WAR

Cole, A. C. *The Irrepressible Conflict, 1850–1865.* New York: Macmillan Co., 1934.

Green, Fletcher M. *Constitutional Development in the South Atlantic States, 1776–1860.* Chapel Hill: University of North Carolina Press, 1930.

Hart, Albert Bushnell. *Slavery and Abolition.* New York: Harper & Brothers, 1906.

Phillips, Ulrich Bonnell (edited by Ellis Merton Coulter). *The Course of the South to Secession.* New York: D. Appleton-Century Co., 1939.

Randall, James G. *Civil War and Reconstruction.* Boston: D. C. Heath & Co., 1953.

Stampp, Kenneth (ed.). *The Causes of the Civil War.* Englewood Cliffs, New Jersey: Prentice-Hall, 1959.

Woodward, C. Vann. *The Burden of Southern History.* Baton Rouge: Louisiana State University Press, 1960.

NATIVISM

Billington, Ray Allen. *Protestant Crusade, 1800–1860.* New York: Rinehart, 1938.

Gordon, Milton M. *Assimilation in American Life.* New York: Oxford University Press, 1964.

Handlin, Oscar. *Race and Nationality in American Life.* Boston: Little, Brown & Co., 1950.

Higham, John. *Strangers in the Land*. New Brunswick: Rutgers University Press, 1955.

Wittke, Carl F. *The Irish in America*. Baton Rouge: Louisiana State University Press, 1956.

PROHIBITION, THE KLAN, AND RURAL AMERICA

Baker, Gordon E. *Rural versus Urban Political Power*. Garden City: Doubleday & Co., 1955.

Editors of Fortune Magazine. *The Exploding Metropolis*. New York: Doubleday & Co., 1958.

Gusfield, Joseph R. *Symbolic Crusade: Status Politics and the American Temperance Movement*. Urbana: University of Illinois Press, 1963.

Hofstadter, Richard. *The Age of Reform*. New York: Alfred A. Knopf, 1955.

Odegard, Peter H. *Pressure Politics: The Story of the Anti-Saloon League*. New York: Columbia University Press, 1928.

Rice, Arnold S. *The Ku Klux Klan in American Politics*. Washington: Public Affairs Press, 1962.

LONG, COUGHLIN, AND THE THIRTIES

Kane, Harnett T. *Louisiana Hayride*. New York: W. Morrow & Co., 1941.

Roche, John P. *The Quest for the Dream*. New York: Macmillan Co., 1963. (Also useful for all subsequent topics.)

Sindler, Allan P. *Huey Long's Louisiana*. Baltimore: Johns Hopkins Press, 1956.

Strong, Donald S. *Organized Anti-Semitism in America*. Washington: American Council on Public Affairs, 1941.

Swing, Raymond Gram. *Forerunners of American Fascism*. New York: Julian Messner, 1935.

MC CARTHYISM

Lubell, Samuel. *The Future of American Politics*. Garden City: Doubleday & Co., 1956.

Rovere, Richard. *Senator Joe McCarthy*. New York: Harcourt, Brace & Co., 1959.

Stouffer, Samuel A. *Communism, Conformity, and Civil Liberties*. Garden City: Doubleday & Co., 1955.

THE NEGRO

Brink, William, and Louis Harris. *The Negro Revolution in America*. New York: Simon and Schuster, 1964.

Grimes, Alan P. *Equality in America*. New York: Oxford University Press, 1964.

Humphrey, Hubert H. (ed.). *School Desegregation*. New York: Thomas Y. Crowell Co., 1964.

King, Martin Luther, Jr. *Stride Toward Freedom*. New York: Harper & Brothers, 1958.

Mendelson, Wallace. *Discrimination*. Englewood Cliffs, New Jersey: Prentice-Hall, 1962.

Myrdal, Gunnar. *An American Dilemma*. New York: Harper & Brothers, 1944.

Tumin, Melvin M. *Desegregation: Resistance and Readiness*. Princeton: Princeton University Press, 1958.

Woodward, C. Vann. *The Strange Career of Jim Crow*. New York: Oxford University Press, 1955.

RELIGIOUS FRICTION

Barker, Ernest. *Church, State and Education*. Ann Arbor: University of Michigan Press, 1957.

Forster, Arnold, and Benjamin R. Epstein. *Some of My Best Friends*. New York: Farrar, Straus and Cudahy, 1962.

Littell, Franklin H. *From State Church to Pluralism*. Garden City: Doubleday & Co., 1962.

Manwaring, David. *Render unto Caesar*. Chicago: University of Chicago Press, 1962.

Marty, Martin. *The New Shape of American Religion*. New York: Harper & Brothers, 1959.

Moore, Edmund A. *A Catholic Runs for President*. New York: Ronald Press, 1956.

Murray, John Courtney. *We Hold These Truths*. New York: Sheed & Ward, 1960.

BIBLIOGRAPHY

Myers, Gustavus. *A History of Bigotry in the United States.* New York: Random House, 1943.

Oaks, Dallin H. (ed.). *The Wall Between Church and State.* Chicago: University of Chicago Press, 1963.

Odegard, Peter H. (ed.). *Religion and Politics.* New York: Oceana Publications, 1960.

Stedman, Murray S., Jr. *Religion and Politics in America.* New York: Harcourt, Brace & World, 1964.

Underwood, Kenneth W. *Protestant and Catholic.* Boston: Beacon Press, 1957.

THE RADICAL RIGHT

Adorno, Theodore, *et al. The Authoritarian Personality.* New York: Harper & Brothers, 1950.

Bell, Daniel (ed.). *The Radical Right.* Garden City: Doubleday & Co., 1963.

Broyles, J. Allen. *The John Birch Society: Anatomy of a Protest.* Boston: Beacon Press, 1964.

Forster, Arnold, and Benjamin R. Epstein. *Danger on the Right.* New York: Random House, 1964.

Hoffer, Eric. *The True Believer.* New York: Harper & Brothers, 1951.

Lens, Sidney. *The Futile Crusade: Anti-Communism as American Credo.* Chicago: Quadrangle Books, 1964.

Overstreet, Harry and Bonaro. *The Strange Tactics of Extremism.* New York: W. W. Norton & Co., 1964.

FOREIGN POLICY AND CONSENSUS

Agar, Herbert. *The Price of Power.* Chicago: University of Chicago Press, 1957.

Almond, Gabriel. *The American People and Foreign Policy.* New York: Harcourt, Brace & Co., 1950.

Carleton, William G. *The Revolution in American Foreign Policy.* New York: Random House, 1963.

Halle, Louis J. *Civilization and Foreign Policy.* New York: Harper & Brothers, 1955.

Halle, Louis J. *Men and Nations.* Princeton: Princeton University Press, 1962.

Kennan, George F. *Realities of American Foreign Policy*. Princeton: Princeton University Press, 1954.

Morgenthau, Hans J. *Dilemmas of Politics*. Chicago: University of Chicago Press, 1958.

Morgenthau, Hans J. *The Purpose of American Politics*. New York: Alfred A. Knopf, 1960.

Ransom, Harry Howe. *Can American Democracy Survive Cold War?* Garden City: Doubleday & Co., 1964.

Spanier, John. *American Foreign Policy Since World War II*. New York: Praeger, 1960.

INDEX

Africa: 27, 32

Alabama: economic growth in, 72; mentioned, 52

Alien Act of 1798: 29, 50

amendments, constitutional. SEE Constitution, U. S., Amendment of

America First Committee: extremist infiltration of, 59

American Communist Party: effectiveness of, 90

Americanism: of Radical Right, 83

American Nazi Party: 59

American Party. SEE Know-Nothings (American Party)

American Revolution. SEE Revolution, American

anarchist: 8, 11, 42

anarchy: 6, 7

Anglo-Saxon: America as, 53; American usage of term, 53 n.; mentioned, 54

anti-Catholicism. SEE Catholicism

Anti-Federalists: struggle of, against federal supremacy, 21–22; effect of Jefferson administration on, 22

anti-Semitism: in colonial America, 28; against Jewish immigrants, 52; of Ku Klux Klan, 54; of Father Coughlin and groups in 1930's, 58–59; and McCarthy, 61; decline of, in America, 76; in Radical Right, 80

armed forces. SEE military, the

Army, U.S.: McCarthy's attacks on, 62

Articles of Confederation: state-federal relation in, 21, 44

Australia: 40

automation: 71

Birchers, John. SEE John Birch Society

Black Codes: 49

Black Muslims: rejection of American society by, 35; danger of, and Negro leadership, 73

Bohemia: immigrants from, 31

British Empire. SEE England

Brown v. Board of Education: results of, 70

bureaucrats: in policy formation and administration, 9

Calhoun, John C.: position of, on state-federal relationship, 23, 44

Canada: 19, 24, 40

capitalism: necessity of, in political system, 39; Radical Right position on, 81–82

Catholicism: opposition to, in colonial America, 28; in acceptance of immigrants, 30, 50–51; Know-Nothing opposition to, 50–51; Ku Klux Klan hatred of, 54; in American concept of Anglo-Saxon, 53 n.; responsibility of, for cultural changes, 55; as religion of McCarthy, 61; and decline of anti-Catholicism, 75–76; mentioned, 37. SEE ALSO Coughlin, Father

Central Africa: 27

China: acceptance of immigrants from, 32, 36, 54

—, Red: containment of, in U.S. foreign policy, 86; criticism of Soviet policy in, 86–87; military power of, 87; response of, to nuclear war threat, 87

Christianity: in America, 37; Radical Right position on, 82–83

Christian Front: anti-Semitism of, 58

cities: Negro movement to, 49, 68; immigrant settlements in, 52. SEE ALSO urbanization

citizens. SEE public, U.S.

citizenship. SEE consensus on membership in political system; political participation; voting

civil disobedience: in theologically based political theories, 4, 5; in natural-law political philosophy, 5; nature theory of, 12; and denial of political rights, 12; and morally significant issues, 12–13; effect of, on stability of society, 12–13. SEE ALSO civil disturbances; rebellion; revolution

civil disturbances: and acceptance of Negro, 72–74

civil servants: in policy formation and administration, 9

Civil War: as failure of unity, 15, 92; slavery as issue in, 37; effect of, on country, 43–44, 45; in settling Negro status, 48; Negro problem as legacy of, 48–50; mentioned, 31, 46, 50, 51, 55

— state-federal-relation issue in: as disagreement on basic character of political system, 19; nature of, 21–22; extent of settlement of, 23; and nationalism in Civil War, 44–55; as continuing problem, 44–45, 47, 48–50; Southern position on, as self-defeating, 45

Cleveland, Grover: 63

Clinton, George: 21

Cold War: criticism of policies of, 86–87

Committee on Civil Rights (President Truman's): 69

Common Market, European: 46

Communism: McCarthy attack on, 61; and Radical Right on foreign policy, 80–81; mentioned 20. SEE ALSO China, Red; Soviet Union

— in America: failure of, among Negroes, 35; and unions supporting McCarthy, 61; and rightist opposition to Negro, 80; as threat to consensus, 89–90; effectiveness of, 90

Communist Party (U.S.): and McCarthy, 61; effectiveness of, 90. SEE ALSO Communism in America

consensus, national: place of criticism and disagreement in, 4, 13, 36–37, 41, 88–89, 90–91, 93, 95; success in maintaining, 13, 92; internal and external threats to, 14–15; unifying forces in, 14–16; after Kennedy assassination, 91–92; as necessary to all political systems, 93–94; necessity of, 93–95; as justification of democracy, 93; elements necessary to future, 94–95

—, challenges to: importance of understanding, 66; capacity to deal with, 89; potential danger of, 89; need for awareness and actions on, 92–93. SEE ALSO consensus, future challenges to; consensus, past challenges to; consensus, present challenges to

— on basic character of system: necessity of, 18–19, 41, 43; state-federal relation in, 19, 21–23, 26, 44–48, 49–50; democracy in, 21, 23–26; and disagreement on specific policies, 36–37, 38, 88–89, 90–91; and extremists' desire to alter, 56–57, 59, 60–65, 79–85, 89–91; and McCarthyism, 60–65; and extremists of left, 89–91; and Kennedy assassination, 91–92

—, future challenges to: on basic character of system, 26, 95; on membership of political system, 34–35, 95; on specific policies, 38–39, 40, 95

— on membership in political system:

litical obligation in, 3–4; theories
of political obligation in, 4–7; See
also political obligation

political science. See political philosophy

political system: requisites for
healthy, 18–19, 26, 36–37, 43;
French, 20; symptoms of unhealthy, 17–18, 41–42. See also
political system, U.S.

—, challenges to. See consensus, challenges to; consensus, future challenges to; consensus, past challenges to; consensus, present challenges to

—, character of, basic. See consensus,
on basic character of system; democracy; Constitution, U.S.; government, federal, relation of to
state government

—, consensus in. See consensus

—, government of. See government,
federal; government, municipal;
government, state

—, membership in. See consensus, on
membership in system; immigrants; Negro, the

—, policies of. See consensus, on specific policies; economy, U.S.; foreign policy; moral issues; policy,
U.S.

—, political leaders of. See extremists; political leaders; politicians

—, political participation in. See political participation; public, U.S.:
voting

—, political parties in. See political
parties

politicians: in policy formation and
administration, 9; in relation of
public and government, 9; avoid-
ance of religious and moral issues
by, 37; Southern, in arguing
states' rights, 46; mentioned, 56.
See also political leaders

population, U.S.: size and diversity

of, 13–14; related to acceptance of
immigrants, 28, 29; mentioned,
26

Porter, David (admiral): 45

President, U.S.: original selection of,
as undemocratic, 24. See also
elections, presidential; Eisenhower, Dwight D.; Fillmore, Millard; Jackson, Andrew; Jefferson,
Thomas; Johnson, Lyndon B.;
Kennedy, John F.; Lincoln, Abra-
ham; Roosevelt, Franklin D.; Truman, Harry S.; Wilson, Woodrow

press, freedom of: 81

Prohibition: as religious and moral
issue, 37

Protestantism: as dominant in U.S.,
50; in American concept of Anglo-
Saxon, 53 n.; and McCarthy's attacks on clergy, 61; mentioned, 37,
54

public, U.S.: role of, in government,
8–12; influence of, on judiciary,
25–26; religiousness of, 37–38;
mobility of, 47–48; effect of Mc-
Carthyism on, 63–64; reaction of,
to Kennedy assassination, 91–92.
See also political obligation; political participation; voting rights

Puerto Ricans: membership of, in
American political system, 27, 36

Quakers: 28

Quebec, Canada: 27

race isue: Huey Long's use of, 56–
57; effect of McCarthy on, 64; federal action on, 69–70; effect of
organized religion on, 77. See
also Negro; racial groups; racism;
segregation, racial

racial groups: variety of, in U.S., 26;
rejections of, in U.S., 32–36. See
also Negro; race issue; racism;
segregation, racial

racism: of Ku Klux Klan, 54, 56; of

This book may be kept

FOURTEEN DAYS

A fine will be charged for each day the book
is kept over time.
